BEAGLE

MIRIAM FIELDS-BABINEAU

Beagle

Editor: Mary E. Grangeia
Copy Editor: Ellen Bingham
Indexer: Elizabeth Walker
Series Design: Mary Ann Kahn
Designer: Patricia Escabi

TFH Publications®
President/CEO: Glen S. Axelrod
Executive Vice President: Mark E. Johnson
Publisher: Christopher T. Reggio
Production Manager: Kathy Bontz

TFH Publications, Inc.®
One TFH Plaza
Third and Union Avenues
Neptune City, NJ 07753

Discovery Communications, Inc. Book Development Team: Marjorie Kaplan, President and General Manager, Animal Planet Media / Kelly Day, EVP and General Manager, Discovery Commerce / Elizabeth Bakacs, Vice President, Licensing and Creative / JP Stoops, Director, Licensing / Bridget Stoyko, Associate Art Director

Printed and bound in China

11 12 13 14 15 16   1 3 5 7 9 8 6 4 2

Library of Congress Cataloging-in-Publication Data
Fields-Babineau, Miriam.
  Beagle / Miriam Fields-Babineau.
     p. cm.
  Includes index.
  ISBN 978-0-7938-3722-9 (alk. paper)
  1. Beagle (Dog breed) I. Title.
  SF429.B3F54 2011
  636.753'7--dc22
                            2011006983

This book has been published with the intent to provide accurate and authoritative information in regard to the subject matter within. While every reasonable precaution has been taken in preparation of this book, the author and publisher expressly disclaim responsibility for any errors, omissions, or adverse effects arising from the use or application of the information contained herein. The techniques and suggestions are used at the reader's discretion and are not to be considered a substitute for veterinary care. If you suspect a medical problem consult your veterinarian.

Note: In the interest of concise writing, "he" is used when referring to puppies and dogs unless the text is specifically referring to females or males. "She" is used when referring to people. However, the information contained herein is equally applicable to both sexes.

The Leader In Responsible Animal Care for Over 50 Years!®
www.tfh.com

CONTENTS

ORIGINS OF
YOUR BEAGLE

In February of 2008, Uno the Beagle won Best in Show at the Westminster Dog Show held at Madison Square Garden in New York City. It was the first time in history that a Beagle won this prestigious title. Yet, Beagles have been a favored dog breed in the United States for more than 100 years. Charles Schultz immortalized them with his cartoon character, Snoopy, the canine buddy of Charlie Brown, in his well-renowned comic strip *Peanuts*. So, it was about time that the Beagle was finally recognized as one of the most perfect dogs in the United States! Uno created such a stir with his confidence, spunk, and perfect appearance that the judge had no choice but to agree with the roaring crowd.

Uno's win at Westminster was also significant because it gave homage to the "everyday dog": a devoted companion who may not be glamorous but who is affectionate, hard-working, easy to care for, and great with children. Although Beagles were originally bred to hunt small game and are still used in this capacity, they also have earned a solid reputation as wonderful, entertaining pets who want nothing more than to spend time with their family pack—well, and have an occasional romp in search of an interesting scent.

HISTORY OF THE BREED

Scenthounds have been aiding hunters for thousands of years. They were used by the ancient Assyrians, Babylonians, and Egyptians to track game. Some historical records exist stating that Beagle-type dogs were used in Ancient Greece around the 5th century BCE. Greek historian Xenophon's treatise on hunting, called *The Cynegeticus*, refers to a scenthound-type dog who tracked hares as human hunters followed behind on foot. The book also discusses the breeding and training of these hounds for the sport of hunting a variety of game animals. The Romans, too, were known to have used hounds for hunting and sport and as sentries and messengers.

Although the actual origins of the Beagle remain obscure, there are accounts of hunting with packs of hounds in Celtic Britain long before the Romans invaded. When the Romans arrived, they brought with them their Castorian and Fulpine hounds, which were then bred with the indigenous Agassaei breed that was already present in England.

Later historical records show that the Beagle was an established hunting hound at the time of the Crusades. In the 1500s, hounds became more specialized, and the first true Beagle-type dogs were created. Hunters would utilize packs of smaller, more compact hounds to track rabbits, pheasants, quails, and other small animals.

The name Beagle may derive from the French term "begle" meaning "gape throated." This likely referred to the baying sound the dogs made when on a

game trail. Or, it may have originated due to the dog's size because the Celtic name for small and of little worth is "beag"—although "beag" referred not to the dog but the game itself, which was of little worth as it was the commoner's catch of rabbits and hares and not the bigger game sought by the aristocracy and royals in sport.

BEAGLE DEVELOPMENT IN ENGLAND

Several different hounds were used to create what later became the modern Beagle. The first dog of note was the Talbot Hound, brought to Britain by William the Conqueror, also known as The Duke of Normandy, a title he inherited at the age of seven. He was the first Norman King of England, having led the Norman invasion from France with the aid of hired armies from areas of Brittany, Italy, Norwegian territories, and Flanders.

Beagles belong to a class of dogs called hounds, specifically scenthounds.

The reason behind this import of the Talbot Hound was William's enjoyment of hunting, which the plentiful forests of England provided.

The Talbot Hound was a scenthound, like the modern Beagle, and likely derived from the Saint Hubert Hound, which had its origins in 8th century France. Saint Hubert Hounds were much like modern Bloodhounds, bred for scenting and locating large game, though they were slow and bulky. The Talbot Hound was solid white and used for hunting stags and wild boars. The two breeds offered great scenting abilities, but their offspring were still slow moving.

Greyhound genetics were added to the hunting hound to develop more speed and agility, which also added a bit to their size. This combination gave rise to the Southern Hound, which is the closest ancestor to the modern Beagle breed. Over time, the Talbot Hound became extinct in favor of the faster, more agile Southern Hound.

Beagle traits gradually became more refined because hunters wanted a scenthound who primarily tracked hares and rabbits. The tall and solid Southern Hound had good stamina, along with an attractive square head and long, soft ears (much like the modern Beagle), but his body was far too large to quickly track small quarry into the heavy brush that hid their dens. When crossed with the North Country Beagle, a close relation of the Talbot Hound who was smaller with a more pointed muzzle, the result was a faster dog, though one with less highly developed scenting abilities.

Oddly enough, miniature hounds became quite fashionable during medieval times and were a favorite of British royalty, from King Edward II (1302 to 1327) to Queen Elizabeth I (1558 to 1603). At a mere 8 to 9 inches (20 to 23 cm) in height, they could fit inside a pocket or glove, hence the origin of the name "Pocket Beagle." These little dogs were apparently allowed to cavort on top of royal tables during state dinners. They also would often ride along on hunts in their owners' saddlebags and were lowered to the ground to root out small animals from the dense brush, their bay guiding the hunt. Although the standard for the Pocket Beagle was drawn up in 1901, this variety had largely diminished to extinction; genetic lines no longer exist.

The first hunting hounds thought to be ancestors of the Beagle, most notably the Talbot Hound, were brought to Britain by William the Conqueror in the 11th century.

Fox hunting became increasingly popular with the aristocracy during the 18th century, and the fashion again returned to the larger hound breeds because they had the power to chase after and bring down large game. The smaller hounds and wider varieties diminished in favor of these fox-hunting hounds. However, some land owners and farmers maintained packs of the smaller Beagle-type breeds for rabbit hunting and were known to combine them with Foxhound breeds to develop more stamina and speed in them.

THE MODERN BEAGLE IN ENGLAND

Early records dating back to the 1830s state that Reverend Phillip Honeywood, who lived in Essex, England, established a pack of Beagles who were close in appearance to the modern-day Beagle. The details of his breeding program were not officially recorded, but it is believed that he combined North Country

Beagles (remember that during this time the term "Beagle" referred to a small baying hound), Southern Hounds, and Harriers as the main genetic contributors to his pack.

The Honeywood Beagles were small dogs with white coats who stood about 10 inches (25 cm) at the shoulder. A few royal packs also existed at that time, namely those of Prince Albert and Lord Winterton, but the Honeywood Beagles were considered the finest hunting dogs of the three men. Prince Albert and Lord Winterton were more concerned with appearance than performance.

Thomas Johnson, another Beagle breeder, attempted to create dogs who were both attractive and highly capable hunters. He actually developed two separate types of Beagles: One type had a smooth coat, and the other had a broken, or rough, coat. Over time, however, the rough-coated Beagle disappeared in favor of the easier-to-care-for smooth-coated variety that is popular today.

By 1840, the Beagle breed still did not have a recognized standard. Four varieties existed: the Medium Beagle, who still highly resembled the Southern Hound; the Pocket Beagle, who was preferred by royalty and high society; the Fox Beagle, who was basically a smaller version of the Foxhound; and the terrier-type Beagle, who had a rough coat and was a cross between any of the other varieties and what was likely a Scottish Terrier.

Eighteen packs of Beagles were established in England by the 1880s, which removed them from the threat of extinction that had occurred with several other hound breeds earlier that century. In 1891, the already established Masters of Harriers Association added a Beagle section and renamed itself the Association of Masters of Harriers and Beagles. It established the first breed standards, requiring Beagle breeders to maintain specific criteria when creating dogs who were to be registered. That year, 107 packs of Harriers and 40 packs of Beagles were registered. The club held its first show in Peterborough, Britain, in 1896.

By 1902, as the breed enjoyed growing popularity with hunters of small game, the number of registered Beagle packs in England rose to 44. This marked their ascent into the domain of favored companion pets, both in England and abroad.

BEAGLE DEVELOPMENT IN THE UNITED STATES

Beagles are known to have been in America for a long time, arriving with the early settlers. However, no care was given to their breeding, and they were never as attractive as those varieties bred in Britain. It was not until General Richard Rowett of Illinois took an interest in improving the breed that breeding records and standardizations were initialized.

Born in England in 1830, Rowett had been familiar with Beagles as a child. At the age of 21, he migrated to America and lived in Indiana for three years, until the Civil War broke out in 1861. He served as Captain of the 7th Volunteer Infantry, becoming a highly decorated soldier who quickly climbed the ranks to Adjutant General. After the war, he was voted into the Thirteenth General Assembly representing Macoupin County, Illinois. He continued to climb the political and social ladder and was appointed Internal Revenue Commissioner for the Fourth District by President Garfield.

At the start of his civil service career, Rowett developed a 200-acre farm in Carlinville, Illinois, where he bred Thoroughbred horses and created the first American line of standardized Beagles. One of his horses, Spokane, won the Kentucky Derby in 1889. His Beagles made history as well, for he imported several breeding pairs from England and created a more attractive show-quality American Beagle who had excellent conformation as well as strong hunting ability. Captain Richard Rowett was one of three men who drafted the American standard of the breed for the bench and show rings. The American Kennel Club (AKC) recognized the Beagle breed in 1885.

Beagles are known to have been in America for a long time, arriving with the early settlers.

Between the end of the 19th century and the middle of the 20th century, the breed was narrowed down from four varieties to two. Per the standard, the two varieties differ mainly in size—the 13-inch (33 cm) and the 15-inch (38 cm)—but can be any combination of colors: tri-color, black or brown and white, or tan and white.

Though a Beagle won Best in Show at Crufts in 1959, proving the overall popularity of the breed in England, it took another 50 years for this to occur in the United States, with K-Run's Park Me in First, aka Uno, winning Best in Show at Westminster in 2008.

Beagles have been one of America's favorite breeds for over 30 years, ranking in the top ten positions in the AKC listing of breed registrations. In fact, they ranked number one from 1953 through 1959—proving them to be an icon as American as baseball and apple pie!

NATIONAL BEAGLE CLUB OF AMERICA

Besides being a very high-ranking breed in the AKC, Beagles have their own national registry, the National Beagle Club (NBC), which maintains the breed standard as set by the originators of the modern breed in both the conformation and the performance arenas. The standard guides judges in the selection of the best representatives of the breed so that breeders will strive to maintain the highest level of conformation.

The NBC also works to encourage hunting with hounds, the use for which they were originally intended. It is responsible for approving field trial rules as promulgated by the AKC, and it provides registration services for hare and rabbit hunting packs located in the United States and Canada.

HISTORY OF THE NBC

The first Beagle specialty club, the American-English Beagle Club (AEBC), was founded at approximately the same time as the AKC in 1884. It was established by breeders in the Philadelphia area. In 1887, the National Beagle Club (NBC) also was formed with the intention of holding field trials and improving Beagle performance as well as appearance. Initially, the NBC was refused AKC recognition as a sanctioned club due to the existence of the already-established AEBC. Eventually, the two clubs merged, thereafter known as the NBC.

The objective of the NBC was to hold field trial events so that breeders would be encouraged to breed for hunting qualities as well as conformation. The first sanctioned field trial was held in New Hampshire in 1891, with Dual Ch. Frank Forest becoming the winner and major influence of Beagle breeding goals. However, most of the dogs being bred at that time still had the "crooked-legged" appearance they inherited from their Dachshund relatives. So, in 1896, James Kernochan, Master of Hempstead Beagles, imported some English Beagles, which introduced the sounder, tougher appearance of a good hunting dog, also helping to set the Beagle type.

Prior to 1912, Beagle field trials were held primarily in New England, until the events became so large that it was difficult to find an appropriate venue. By 1936, the club was administering an ever-larger contingent of field trial clubs and activities, so they had to establish the Beagle Advisory Commission with the purpose of organizing and superintending these events.

As a result, the NBC Specialty show was moved to Aldie, Virginia, in 1970. The Institute Farm hosted this event and shares an extensive history with the club as well. Five members of the NBC formed a company, the Institute Corporation, in 1916 in order to purchase 508 acres in Aldie for use by the club, particularly to hold their field trials. The land is still owned by the Institute Corporation, which leases it to the Institute Foundation, which in turn maintains the property for the NBC. This land is known as The Institute Farm. The Institute Farm is still used as the site for many NBC activities, including Fall Pack Trials for Basset Hounds and Beagles, AKC field trials, AKC-licensed specialty shows for Beagles, and the annual NBC Triple Challenge Trial.

There are currently approximately 400 regular members, nearly 200 supporting members, and numerous associate members. With the breed's continued rise in popularity, in no small part propagated by the 2008 win of Uno at the Westminster Dog Show, the NBC continues to grow.

REGIONAL SPECIALTY CLUBS

There are numerous clubs in the United States dedicated to Beagle activities and breeding. The following is a partial list:
• Columbia-Willamette Beagle Club (based in Portland, OR)
  www.cwbeagles.com
• Phoenix Arizona Beagle Club
  www.phxazbeagleclub.com
• Rocky Mountain Beagle Club (based in Denver, CO)
  www.rockymountainbeagleclub.com
• San Jacinto Beagle Club (based in Houston, TX)
  www.sanjacintobeagleclub.org
• Southern California Beagle Club (based in Los Angeles, CA)
  www.socalbeagle.org
• South Kentucky Beagle Club (based in London, KY)
  www.southkybeagleclub.com
• Southern New York Beagle Club, Inc. (based in Yorktown Heights, NY)
  www.akc.org/akc_clubs/?SouthernNewYorkBeagleClub
• Wisconsin Beagle Club (based in Madison, WI)
  www.akc.org/akc_clubs/?WisconsinBeagleClubInc
  To obtain a full listing of Beagle clubs, go to www. clubs.akc.org/NBC or try this link: www.barkbytes.com/clubs/beagle.htm

BEAGLE RESCUES

As Beagles are much loved but not always understood, there are many rescue organizations that foster them until they are able to find forever homes. Should you wish to adopt a Beagle, try contacting a rescue group. The following are some web links to regional groups that sponsor adoption programs:
• American Kennel Club: www.akc.org/breeds/rescue.cfm#B
• Mid-Atlantic and Upper Mid-West: www.brewbeagles.org
• New Boston, NH: www.bonesbeagles.org

Specialty clubs are an integral part of the dog fancy, maintaining breed standards and sponsoring breed shows and performance trials.

- Littleton, CO: www.colobeaglerescue.org
- TN, AL, and NJ: www.sosbeagles.org
- NC: www.tribeagles.org
- Tampa, FL: www.tampabaybeaglerescue.org
- Portland, OR and Yardley, PA: www.cascaderescue.org
- Atlanta, GA: www.atlantabeaglerescue.org

A TOP-TEN DOG

Although AKC dog registration statistics have made the little Beagle's current popularity official with his top-ten status, he has been our constant companion for millennia: as a hunting partner, tireless on the trail; as an elite companion of royalty, cavorting at their tables and sitting as the regal subject of numerous portraits, his coloring and pleasing conformation attractive to depict; and as a faithful, loving, clown-like pet, living with us in our homes and playing with our children. Beagles are easily recognized, much loved, and a perennial favorite among dog lovers worldwide.

CHARACTERISTICS
OF YOUR BEAGLE

In the *Peanuts* comic strip, Snoopy is intelligent, inventive, and loyal, although it's quite clear he has his own agenda. Yet, the personality traits of this fictional canine are not far from the truth. Even Snoopy's preference for sleeping on top of his dog house can often be observed in real-life Beagles, though few of them are Flying Aces.

Beagles are great family dogs and are generally very gentle with children. Being pack animals, they do well with other dogs and thrive in busy households. In fact, they are best suited to active families because they are an active breed. Most hunting dogs were bred to work, and a scenthound such as the Beagle requires a constant outlet for his energy.

Beagles are easy to care for. They are rarely picky about what they eat, they have short coats for easy grooming, and they are very hardy dogs. These attributes are great for beginner dog owners looking for an easygoing, uncomplicated, and enthusiastic companion whose needs are easily met.

Highly adaptable, the breed's compact size allows for a comfortable adjustment to most environments. If you live in a complex that allows only small dogs, Beagles will fit in nicely. Live in the country? Beagles love to romp through fields and woods, making this another perfect environment for the breed. Whether you are active outdoors or just want to stay home and cuddle with your dog, Beagles are wonderful companions and will learn to fit into any setting. Keep in mind,

Easy to care for, Beagles tend to be friendly, active, and intelligent dogs who make enthusiastic and loyal companions.

however, that all young dogs are filled with energy, and Beagles are no different. Appropriate exercise is conducive to having a well-behaved dog.

BEAGLE PHYSIQUE

Most Beagles have a pleasing, puppy-like appearance for the majority of their lives. They remain roly-poly and have long, silky ears, big brown eyes, and wagging tails. Although they gain size with age, their overall appearance does not change.

BODY

According to the breed standard, the Beagle should appear sturdy, compact, and well balanced.

Beagles are small- to medium-sized dogs. One variety is 13 inches (33 cm) at the top of the shoulder, and the other is 15 inches (38 cm) at the top of the shoulder. Beagles rarely weigh more than 30 pounds (14 kg), with males often being up to 5 pounds (2.3 kg) heavier than females. If the dog weighs more than this, he is likely overweight, which is a very common problem with the breed as these notorious chow hounds will eat almost anything and rarely walk away from food—even when full!

HEAD

Beagles have a long head that tends to be slightly domed on top. Their forehead is broad, and you can often see their skin wrinkling between their ears whenever they are curious or inviting you to play. Their low, silky ears can usually reach the tip of their nose and do not have any erectile ability, other than the muscles at the base that can turn them to aid in detecting sound direction.

Their big, round eyes are generally set well apart and maintain a gentle, soft appearance. Beagle eyes range from hazel to brown; blue eyes, although rare, are not unheard of, especially in a dog who might have merle (mottled) coloring.

Poorly bred Beagles might have a flatter skull or a Romanesque type nose. Sometimes, small terrier-like eyes, a throwback to their past ancestors, can be seen. And, along those lines, their ears can sometimes appear shorter than they should and might even have some ability to rise up a bit. However, while these traits may not be preferred in a show ring, this does not mean the dog is less likely to be a good companion.

SHOULDERS, CHEST, AND NECK

Beagles are built to be great scenthounds. Their body is fairly close to the ground, with strong, muscular shoulders; a deep, broad chest; and a medium-length sleek neck. Their long face helps them reach the ground easily to track with wonderful freedom of movement.

HIPS, LEGS, AND FEET

Beagles have strong hips and thighs that are well muscled, offering an abundance of propulsion power. They also have strong stifles and firm hocks that are symmetrical and moderately bent. Their feet are tight and firm. Open feet can be considered a defect. Other defects include cow hocks or hocks that are too straight, as well as lack of hind muscling, which would greatly reduce their propulsion abilities.

BACK, LOIN, AND RIBS

Beagles have a short back, broad loins, and well-sprung ribs that give them an abundance of lung room, which is ideal for long-term tracking. Strong lungs also enhance their ability to scent and to bark, or bray in the case of hounds. The bray is an important part of Beagle character; it is utilized to alert their human hunting companions to both the pack's location and the location of prey. Beagles use different tones of voice, depending on their status: a tone while tracking, a tone when prey is located, and a tone when closing in on their prey. These vocalizations are beneficial to their human hunting companions. Most people who hunt with Beagles do so on foot, so they cannot travel as quickly as hunters who ride horses or recreational vehicles and can reserve their energies for closing in on their quarry. The braying Beagle will let them know where and when the time is right. What better hunting partner can there be?

TAIL

Beagles have a moderately high set tail, which bears a slight curve, though it is not curved over the back as in some breeds such as Huskies or Akitas. It is short in comparison with most hound tails and has a brush of fur on the underside. The American Kennel Club (AKC) considers the tail to have defects if it is too long, inclined forward at the base, or lacking a brush of fur on the underside.

BE AWARE!

Purchasing your Beagle from a professional breeder has many benefits. First of all, you are more likely to get a dog with proper conformation and temperament because only good representatives of the breed are used in professional breeding programs. While all are not champions, the goal is to produce dogs that resemble the breed standard as much as possible. Second, the dog is likely to come with a health guarantee. Professional breeders inoculate, deworm, and have their pups checked by a reputable veterinarian before they are sold, and they do checks on both parents to ensure that they do not pass genetic diseases and other abnormalities on to their offspring. Pups are usually also held by the breeder until they are at least three months old, so they have received some degree of socialization before going to their new homes.

Most puppy mills give little thought to structural soundness and mental health, focusing primarily on the income from each puppy sold. Also, the majority of the parent dogs are kept in small cages with little grooming, medical care, or handling. Because Beagles are such social dogs, this is a horrific situation, and it is likely that these individuals will have emotional as well as health issues.

COAT

Beagles have a medium-length, smooth, double coat. The coarse, hard-lying outercoat quickly sheds out dirt and moisture; however, it tends to acquire a doggy smell if not kept groomed. Beagles are low to the ground, which means their coats absorb smells that you might not want in your home, especially when the coat is wet. Because Beagles are easy to bathe, there's no need to have to put up with this unattractive odor when it occurs.

Easy keepers, Beagles do well with weekly brushing, which helps to remove shedding hair and debris. You rarely have to take your dog to a professional groomer, unless you want to pamper him with a luxury bath. This breed sheds, though, so the more you curry brush the coat, the less dog hair you will find interwoven in your carpets and on the furniture.

Not having fuller, longer coats, Beagles do not fare well in extremely cold temperatures, although they have some body fat for insulation. Because Beagles were originally bred in England, where the temperatures and weather tend to be cool and damp, they can handle these conditions when working but not as well when at rest. For this reason, your pet should be kept indoors, especially when outdoor temperatures are extremely hot or cold.

COLOR

Beagles display a large variety of coat colors, with most being two or three different colors. Early Beagles were mostly or completely white, making them easy to spot in dense forests. This has changed and rarely exists now as Beagles have developed into and conform to their modern breed standards. Most Beagles are tricolor, with a black saddle, a white chest and underbelly, and a brown or tan face, and their short coat sports brown, tan, black, and white. This coloring is still useful when utilizing their hunting abilities or if just going for a hike in the woods. You will usually see your little buddy, if not hear him loud and clear.

Many Beagles have ticking, or freckles, that can be either tan or black, along with patches of color on their body and head. The ticking is mostly along the legs but can manifest anywhere on the torso and tail.

According to the breed standard, both varieties of Beagles can be any combination of hound colors—white, black, tan, lemon (a very light tan), brown, bluish/gray, or reddish brown. All these colors are considered acceptable by the AKC for breed registration and exhibition. With such a variety of coloring, you are sure to have a very unique Beagle. Uno, the Beagle who won Best in Show at the Westminster Dog Show in 2008, is considered a patch coat, with tan patches over a mostly white base coat; a "saddle" over his back, head, and ears; and patches over his eyes, as well as on his tail. Overall, he has a very striking and clear coloring, adding to his perfect conformation and outgoing attitude.

Beagles have a medium-length, smooth double coat that comes in a variety of colors. Most are tricolor, with a black saddle, a white chest and underbelly, and brown or tan faces.

Dog Tale

Beagles love people and enjoy being the center of attention. This makes them great with youngsters and other pets. However, this can sometimes get them into trouble because they might seek to greet someone who is afraid of them or dislikes dogs in general.

I once performed a behavior consultation for a family with a 6-year-old boy, Tyler, who was extremely fearful of dogs. As an infant, he'd had a bad experience with a neighbor's dog and since then was terrified of them, especially when they were barking.

After an initial consultation and discussion about how much the family wanted to have a dog, I brought my Beagle, George, to their home. He is very well-trained and quiet around children, so I hoped Tyler could become desensitized to his anxiety about dogs by spending some time with George. In just two visits, Tyler warmed up to him, seeing that he remained still and did not pose any threats. By the third visit, the boy was extremely happy to see George and greeted him the moment he walked in the door.

It took only four sessions for Tyler to begin asking if George could move in with them. The boy's father asked if he could purchase George, since his son had taken to him so well. Of course, I had to refuse because George was part of my family. However, I helped them pick out a Beagle of their own, and through training, the dog and the boy, who felt greatly empowered with the ability to control the dog, became inseparable.

It is always a good idea to first ask if your dog can greet a small child and then be certain to have your Beagle sitting or lying down when the child wishes to interact with him. Because Beagles love to jump up, this can frighten a youngster. Avoid these types of situations by maintaining control of your Beagle while out on your adventures with him.

LIVING WITH YOUR BEAGLE

The Beagle's easygoing nature, charming and lively personality, and kind heart have made him a highly sought after canine companion for young and old alike. He will happily share your life, wherever you hang your hat, and will most certainly make you smile. All he will require is lots of affection and companionship, daily exercise, and a place to play.

PERSONALITY

Beagles are great family dogs. They are very social, love to play, adore being cuddled, and enjoy family activities. They are very accepting of new people and other pets. In fact, they prefer the company of other animals, and the more people—especially children—the better.

This is not a needy breed. Beagles can play independently, though as with most dogs, they prefer interactive play. They are highly tolerant and forgiving but can be overwhelming for very young children as they are prone to jumping up, mouthing, and excessive noise. Even their fast-moving upright tails can be annoying if a small child is popped in the face enough times.

Beagles can do well in any environment—whether urban, suburban, or rural—but must receive lots of exercise. They are not the ideal pet for someone who works long hours or travels a lot, leaving the dog home alone. A lonely Beagle will bark excessively, and a bored Beagle will become destructive. He may enjoy following a scent and being independent, but he also craves a cohesive pack, which means regular routines and companionship.

Beagles make wonderful family pets but require ample daily exercise to remain fit and happy. An ideal environment includes a fenced-in yard in which to run and play.

ENVIRONMENT

Small and compact, Beagles can adapt well to living in urban environments. However, if you live in a high rise, duplex, or town house, you may not have the option of just letting your dog out the door to exercise in a secure yard. You must take him for walks. He will need at least five potty walks a day, with two of them being long walks for exercise.

It will be impossible for you to walk your Beagle unless you train him; a Beagle will pull hard when he catches an interesting scent or wants to greet someone. This will be frustrating not only for you but also for him. Leash pulling creates tension that can turn into assertive gestures. It can also damage his trachea if he is pulling on a leash attached to a neck collar. Learn about positive training techniques (see Chapter 7), and apply them during all of your dog's outings.

You may live in a concrete jungle, but your Beagle still thinks of it as a scent sensation. Allow him time to be himself and sniff, provided he isn't pulling you down the street. The art of loose leash walking will enable him to be a Beagle while still keeping an eye out for your location without constant tension.

An urban hound will also need to have a regimented and consistent schedule. This will prevent accidents in your home. Because you will likely have to walk your dog down the hall, then traverse stairs, an elevator, and a lobby as well as some amount of sidewalk before reaching his relief area, be sure to make the trek before he is hopping from foot to foot having to potty. Without this foresight, he might have an accident along the way, which would be inconvenient for you and give him the wrong message. It isn't fair to admonish your Beagle for relieving himself on the sidewalk instead of at the park. If you are late in keeping with his schedule, you might be best served by carrying him to his relief area to prevent an accident along the way. Carrying a 25-pound (11-kg) dog a distance can be difficult, but sticking to a consistent schedule is not as hard.

If you cannot take your dog out several times each day due to your work or family schedule, consider either hiring a dog walker or taking him to a doggy daycare center. This way, he will be less likely to have accidents within your home or become overly destructive. Walks will offer relief and exercise. A doggy daycare will offer that as well as socialization, making him far easier to live with when you come home tired after a long day of work. This is especially important for a puppy or young dog. As your Beagle ages, he may not require as much exercise, although it's important to continue with an exercise regimen to maintain his overall health and well-being.

Highly adaptable and small, Beagles can live comfortably in most living environments—from town to country—and especially thrive in busy households.

A dog who lives in a suburban environment will likely have the benefit of a back yard in which to romp. While this is great, it should not be the sole exercise you offer your Beagle. He still prefers to be with you, so taking a walk with him each day will promote the bond between you and enrich his life. There are more scents to discover on a walk through the neighborhood than there are in the yard. If you live near a park that offers walking paths, trails, and streams, allow your Beagle a chance to sniff and run, while keeping him on a long leash. If you cannot do this with him daily, try to do so at least a couple times each week. Also give him time to play with other dogs. People cannot play with dogs the way they play with each other.

If you intend to allow your dog freedom within your back yard, make certain that it is securely fenced. Beagles are skilled escape artists, especially if they catch an irresistible scent. An agile breed, Beagles love to climb, hence Charles Schultz's depiction of Snoopy on top of his dog house more than inside it. If climbing allows them a better view, or escape, they will do so. So, if you don't want your dog to escape your yard, you will need to construct a sturdy, high fence and bury at least a foot (30.5 cm) of it beneath the ground at the base, which is the best means of ensuring his safety and security.

Beagles also love to dig. Digging alleviates boredom as much as it is a means to search out an interesting scent. Do you have moles or rabbits in your yard? Your Beagle is sure to catch their scent and dig wherever they have been. If you thought the holes from these critters were bad, you're not likely to appreciate trenches that travel from hole to hole. The best means of preventing a clash between your ideas of landscaping and your dog's restructuring of that environment is to set up an area that is specifically for him—a place where you aren't worried about what he digs up and where he does it. You can enrich his environment further by supplying climbing structures and piles of sand or dirt for digging purposes. This won't prevent inappropriate digging altogether, however. You will still need to supervise his play time and redirect him to appropriate behavior when he attempts to unearth your flower beds and bushes.

Living with a Beagle in a rural setting is wonderful. Your dog is certain to have many opportunities to be himself and receive exercise. Still keep in mind, however, that he will catch a scent and disappear quickly should he not be monitored and kept on leash. Many dogs have run off and disappeared during a hunt. Much of the time, they are lost forever. The lucky ones survive and are found, but many perish due to exposure and hunger. Even though you may live in the wide open spaces or vast forest, do not allow your Beagle to roam off leash or unmonitored, even if well trained. He will always choose to follow an interesting scent over coming when called, especially if he already has a head start and your voice is in the distance.

TRAINABILITY

Your Beagle buddy may be obstinate, but he is still highly trainable. You will be most successful if you begin training him while he is still very young. A puppy is open to new experiences and will learn quickly. A dog over 3 years of age can

PUPPY POINTER

Beagle puppies learn faster than older dogs do. They will quickly respond to food lures and love to hear praise. They also enjoy being touched and petted, so this also is a great way to reward and reinforce dogs when they behave appropriately. Because pups are always learning by testing their environment, it's a good idea to be consistent with training from the moment you bring your Beagle puppy home. So don't allow undesirable behaviors now that you don't wish your pup to repeat later. If you set the rules early and consistently stick to them, your Beagle pup will learn what is expected of him and be more successful in his training.

By the age of 2 months, your Beagle puppy is able to begin basic training and learn simple commands, including housetraining, sitting and coming readily when called, what he can or cannot chew, and how to walk nicely on a leash. Never believe that your Beagle pup is too young to learn any concept. Positive training will set the foundation for good manners and future learning and prevent problem behaviors before they start.

often be more set in his behavior and not as willing to accept your direction.

Beagles are not usually able to maintain attention on anything for a long period of time, unless it is a scent. They are easily distracted and will become depressed if handled coarsely. They learn best when positive reinforcement is used and consistent routines are put into place. Having a huge food drive makes food rewards most welcome and training more effective. When your dog figures out that he will earn food, he will do anything! Just be sure that you keep the training sessions short enough to maintain his attention and desire to partake in future training.

SUPPLIES FOR YOUR BEAGLE

Your Beagle will need a few belongings to help him acclimate to his new home and family. It is best to obtain the majority of these items prior to bringing him home so that you will be fully prepared and able to make him comfortable right away.

He will need dishes for food and water, a bed of his own, a collar and leash for walks, grooming supplies, and more. You will also need to consider the supplies needed for giving your Beagle appropriate nutrition, training, and safety. The amount and type of supplies will depend largely on where he will live and what your goals might be with him.

Entering a pet shop and trying to figure out exactly which items are necessary can be difficult. This chapter will detail all the information you will need for remaining on target with what your dog most definitely requires and also some items that might be fun for quality time spent with your Beagle buddy.

COLLAR AND HARNESS

Before getting your Beagle, you will need to purchase the items needed to safely transport him from his current location to your home. For this, a collar or harness as well as a leash will be definite requirements. If he is a young pup, though, it's safer to transport him in a crate that is appropriate to his size, one sturdy enough for you to carry and to prevent your pup from injury should the crate slide around a bit in the car. (See the section on crates.) If your new Beagle is too large to carry around in a crate, or you cannot confine him in a crate within your vehicle, then he should be controlled via a collar or harness attached to a leash. The type of tool you use will depend on your Beagle's age and whether or not he has been leash trained.

COLLAR

There are so many collars to choose from, so how do you know which one is right for your dog? Collars are available in leather, nylon, cotton, and chain. If your Beagle is young, he is sure to grow—and rapidly—so consider purchasing a collar that will grow with him. Adjustable collars are available in a vast array of fun patterns and colors. These can be cotton, nylon, or even leather. If your Beagle is fully grown, you can purchase any type of collar, but consider function and safety as well as appearance.

Prior to purchase, measure your dog's neck around the middle. Add 2 inches (5 cm) to get an idea of what size collar you'll need to get. When purchasing an adjustable collar for a puppy, allow an extra 6 inches (15 cm) to accommodate future growth.

Your Beagle will need a few belongings to help him acclimate to his new home and family. Get all of your supplies before bringing your new dog home.

The only types of collars that should be avoided are those made of metal—specifically prong and choke-type collars. Aside from being inhumane and often incorrectly used, this type of collar risks your dog's life and well-being, especially if it is left on at all times. A choke collar, even one made of nylon, can become caught on a fence, deck, crate grate, or even furniture. A panicked dog will pull relentlessly and can become fatally injured due to air restriction and tracheal collapse. Prong collars inflict pain by squeezing your dog's skin between the prongs every time they are pulled. They should never be used on a dog for any reason.

The type of collar you intend to leave on your Beagle should be safe and comfortable. One that has a quick-release clip is generally safe, provided it does not have any means of choking your dog should it become entangled or caught. A quick-release clip will afford you the chance to easily dislodge him. If your Beagle socializes, as he should, this is another chance for collar entanglement. Either remove his collar prior to allowing him to play with other dogs, or maintain a watchful eye to ensure that another dog does not catch his jaw on the collar. Also, be observant for collar damage due to rough play; dogs will chew on each other's collars at times. A damaged collar will not withstand any leash pressure, possibly breaking at the slightest tug.

HARNESS

The best type of containment control for a Beagle more than 3 months old is a front-connecting body harness. A harness won't cause damage to the dog's trachea when pressure is applied. The front connection offers the means of turning your dog back to you should he forge ahead toward distractions, whereas a harness that has a leash connection on the back will merely teach your dog

A collar or harness must be properly fitted for your dog's safety and comfort.

to pull harder, much like a sled dog. So unless you intend to put on some roller skates or stand on a skateboard ready to go for a ride, a front-connecting body harness will be safer and aid in teaching your Beagle to pay attention to you instead of pulling—and it won't cause physical damage to your dog.

When fitting your dog for a harness, consider whether or not he will be growing. If so, you want something that adjusts all the way around. Most harnesses feature universal adjustments and point-of-purchase tags that state the measurements appropriate for that item. As a starting point, measure your Beagle around his abdomen, just behind his front legs. Next, measure him around his chest behind his shoulders. Proper fit is essential because a shifting harness can cause chafing, and a wiggly Beagle might be able to chew on it or remove it.

LEASH

Leashes of all lengths and types will be plentiful on pet store shelves. You will see cotton, nylon, chain, leather, and retractable types, among others. Again, you will face the dilemma of which one to choose for your new Beagle. Each type will help you hold on to your sniffing machine, but not all are equal in usefulness, and some can actually be detrimental to giving your dog the right message, which is to stay near you.

LEATHER

Your first consideration should be your own comfort. How will the leash feel in your hand? Will you be able to maintain a grip on it if your dog pulls or if it gets wet? With this in mind, the safest and most comfortable type of leash is one made of leather. A 6-foot (2-m) leather leash will allow your Beagle plenty of room to meander when allowed to do so. It will also be easy to grip in any weather and will last the longest, provided you don't allow your dog to use it as a chew toy.

NYLON

Nylon leashes may appear strong but can often hurt your hand if your dog pulls. When wet, they can even slip right through your fingers after giving you a nice case of rope burn. So, while often far more attractive than a sturdy leather leash, a nylon leash may not be the best tool for walking a Beagle.

COTTON

A cotton leash will be a bit more comfortable than a nylon leash, though it's not as sturdy as a leather one. More color and pattern choices are available, which is fun, and cotton leashes are less likely to give you rope burn should your Beagle pull away from you. Unlike nylon, you will still be able to maintain a good grip on a wet cotton leash.

CHAIN

A chain leash may be strong but is far more detrimental to controlling your Beagle than is a nylon, cotton, or leather leash. You will be able to hold on to only the handle and not anywhere else. It will also make a lot of noise. Beagles are sensitive to noise, so it's not a great idea to create more meaningless jangling. Your dog will have enough of this from his collar tags, although you can use a tag silencer on them or wrap them in a rubber band to prevent this from occurring.

RETRACTABLE

Most new dog owners gravitate toward retractable leashes. While the idea of these might be attractive—giving the dog more room to roam on leash—they apply constant pressure on the dog unless locked in place. This means your Beagle will feel constant leash pressure and will, in turn, apply the same constant leash pressure to your end—which means he will learn to pull harder on the leash than he might normally. Your Beagle is not trying to be difficult; this is merely a natural reaction to the constant tension. Should you wish to offer your Beagle more room to roam while on leash, purchase a longer cotton leash; they are available in lengths from 10 to 30 feet (3 to 9 m).

IDENTIFICATION

For your Beagle's safety, his collar or harness should carry identification and health certification tags, as well as your contact information. Most collars can host the tags; some can even have contact information sewn or embroidered into the collar material, which ensures that this information remains intact as tags can fall off and become lost or damaged. Nylon collars are normally the type used for sewn-on identification. However, leather collars can have metal identification tags riveted directly into them as well.

CRATE

Another necessary item that you should have prior to bringing home your Beagle is a crate. A crate is not merely a means of safe transport, it's a place your dog can call his own—a place he can sleep or get away from all the hustle and bustle, as well as a place where he can feel safe when nobody is home.

Crates are similar in size and shape to the dens dogs would have in the wild. Canines prefer to feel walls around them because this gives them a sense of security. However, they also prefer being able to maneuver within their dens. If your Beagle is going to sleep in his crate all night and/or spend time in it for part of the day, make certain you provide him with a retreat that has some extra space for him to move a bit. This means a container in which he can stand up, turn around, and lie down comfortably.

There are two distinct types of crates appropriate for Beagles: metal or solid plastic with front and side grates. Some metal crates come with convenient slide-out metal pans and/or base grates for particulate to pass through to the bottom. Either type of crate should be fine, but if you plan on traveling by air, choose a solid plastic crate that is airline approved.

Your dog's crate will serve many purposes and aid in your dog's mental well-being and your sanity. Young dogs have a tendency to investigate their new surroundings by using their mouths. If you are not able to quickly redirect your Beagle to the appropriate chew objects, you are sure to lose some personal

A crate provides a safe place for your Beagle to stay when you are not at home or when you cannot supervise him.

belongings as well as incur damage to furniture. To prevent inappropriate chewing, you will need to put your Beagle into his crate when you cannot watch him until he is trained. Be sure to give him a special food-filled toy when you do so that he always has positive associations with going into his crate. However, never keep your dog in his crate for long periods of time. He needs to learn about the world and exercise in order to grow up healthy and strong.

PUPPY POINTER

While your Beagle is still a young pup, you may want to restrict your bedding purchase to something that is not stuffed with foam. A soft, spongy mattress is far too attractive for chewing puppies and might end up in bits and pieces everywhere. Opt instead for a flat mat that contains minimal fiber fill and will not be as attractive to chew. When your dog is over his teething period at 9 months, and more respectful of his and your belongings, you can purchase that big stuffed bed for him.

If you have other animals, you can feed your Beagle in his crate until he is settled in and more secure with his pack. This will ensure that he eats only his food and that other animals don't share it either. Feeding your dog in his crate enhances the positive ambiance of the area, making him feel more comfortable in it. If you are teaching your Beagle to ride in your vehicle, time in his crate beforehand will help him adjust and feel more confident with the sounds and movement of the vehicle.

Housetraining will be far easier by incorporating the crate. Because dogs rarely relieve themselves in their dens, it will teach your Beagle to control his relief needs and learn the potty schedule faster. Crating your Beagle when you cannot observe him will prevent numerous potty accidents within your home, thus ensuring that he will remain on your Best in Show list. Young Beagles have a difficult time controlling their urination needs, especially when excited. Crating will help tremendously.

BED

Unless you intend on having your Beagle sleep in your bed, you will need to provide him with one of his own. Initially, you can place cozy bedding like a folded old blanket inside his crate. This will make his den more comfortable and help him learn to identify with his own bed in the future.

When choosing a bed, aim for something that is easily cleaned. Beagles love to play outdoors and are sure to track a good amount of dirt in on the bed. A bed with an easy-to-remove cover, or one flexible enough to put into the washing machine, will save you lots of time and money.

There are several reasons to make certain your Beagle sleeps in his own bed. First of all, because he is a hunting dog, he will most definitely have an odor. He is close to the ground and loves to sniff at it. He will get dirt on his stomach, paws, nose, and often the rest of his body as well, especially if allowed free run in a fenced yard. Second, some Beagles may begin to claim ownership of your bed if they are allowed to sleep there. Ownership means that your dog might want your bed for himself at all times, or he might bring his toys to bed with him, further crowding you to the edge of the mattress.

Dogs do not accept equal partnership of the master bed. Your Beagle will be just as happy, and you even happier, learning to use his own bed.

FOOD AND WATER BOWLS

Your Beagle will need food and water bowls. Even if you already have other dogs who have bowls, your Beagle will need to eat out of his very own. The type you choose should be sturdy, easy to clean, and virtually indestructible. Beagles can be hard on their dishes.

While Snoopy rarely took his food dish on his Flying Ace adventures, it was still used for purposes other than holding his meals. You can count on your Beagle to

Stainless steel bowls are sturdy, easy to clean, and virtually indestructible.

be equally inventive. The dish will be a toy, a dirt receptacle, an object with which to wage battle, and a means of garnering your attention when you least expect it.

You will look at beautiful ceramic dishes, attractive plastic dishes, and stainless steel dishes. If you wish to make a wise purchase from the start, ignore all the glitz and glamour of the breakable dishes and purchase the stainless steel ones. They are now available in some attractive patterns and colors, making it easier to opt for the correct choice.

A ceramic dish is easily broken when taken on your Beagle's adventures, and the glaze may be toxic. Broken pieces can endanger your little sniffer. Plastic dishes can be mistaken for chew toys, also ending up with sharp edges and broken pieces. Stainless steel dishes withstand all the challenges your Beagle will throw at them. Moreover, they are easy to clean, will maintain their shape well, and will be easy to locate in the yard, even if covered in dirt after your Beagle has attempted to bury them.

Your Beagle will need one bowl for food and one for water. It's also a good idea to have two sets of bowls on hand so that you can provide clean bowls daily.

GROOMING SUPPLIES

You won't need much in the way of grooming supplies for your Beagle pup. His coat is wash and wear. No need for clippers and fancy shears or frequent trips to the groomer, unless he likes to roll in nasty-smelling things.

A massage glove (hound mitt) will be helpful in loosening dead hair and will make him feel good at the same time. Who doesn't love a massage? Beagles certainly do! A curry brush works well during periods of heavy shedding. A deodorizing canine shampoo should also be purchased so that you can bathe your Beagle after he's had fun in the yard or out in the woods. Bi-weekly bathing is usually sufficient. Due to your Beagle having folded-over ears that do not allow adequate air circulation, a good herbal ear cleaner should also be on hand and used weekly.

Nail clippers are essential because dogs need to have their nails trimmed every six weeks. There are two main types: guillotine and scissors style. Either type will work when your Beagle is young. However, guillotine clippers will be easier to use when he is an adult and has harder nails.

Good dental hygiene is also important. Don't forget a canine toothbrush and toothpaste. Canine toothbrushes have advanced over the past years. Three-sided brushes offer simultaneous brushing of the front and back of the teeth for a thorough cleaning. Also available are electric canine toothbrushes, but your Beagle will need time to acclimate before you can use one. Finger brushes are easy to use, as are dental wipes. Canine toothpastes come in a variety of flavors and are made specifically for dogs; human varieties can make your dog sick if ingested.

TOYS

Beagles need toys. They are active, creative dogs who will turn anything into a toy if not guided consistently into playing only with their own appropriate play items. Keep in mind, however, that Beagles can be aggressive chewers and destructive of toys that aren't designed for this kind of wear and tear.

Purchase at least six toys for your Beagle. All of them should be indestructible and safe enough for a medium to large dog who exerts fairly strong jaw pressure. Here's a list of some good options:

• Chew toys. Edible and nonedible chew toys come in a large variety of types, sizes, and flavors and are designed to meet the varying needs of every type of chewer. They also promote good canine dental hygiene while enhancing mental fitness and encouraging appropriate chewing.

• Interactive toys. These are sturdy, bouncy, rubber chew toys that can be filled with food treats. They're great for keeping your dog entertained while offering necessary mental stimulation. Your Beagle can safely chew them, so you don't need to worry that you'll find rubber particles on the floor or in his mouth after he's had some fun.

Toys provide excellent opportunities for exercise, mental stimulation, and interaction between pets and their owners.

Dog Tale

Taking your canine companion with you when shopping for pet supplies can be lots of fun—and a rewarding experience for both you and your dog.

I often take my Beagle to a big pet store to practice training basic commands. The best aisles to practice in are the ones lined with dog toys. Not only are all the toys attractive, but this area of the store tends to be the most populated by both people and their dogs, so there are lots of distractions.

For example, to work on training the *stay* command, I pick up toys, throw them in the air, squeak them, or toss them back into their bins. This offers a fun and effective means of teaching your dog to remain focused on you as he learns to maintain his *stay*—regardless of how tempting the possibility of playing with the toys may be! Of course, before leaving the store, I will offer my Beagle a chance to choose a new toy to bring home. Releasing him from work, I allow him to sniff and investigate some of the items he had shown an interest in during distraction training. When he chooses the toy he wants, I allow him to carry it to the register for checkout.

Not only does this experience teach your dog to work well in busy, distraction-filled environments, but he gets to go on an adventure and earn a new toy that he can take home for some more fun.

Before embarking on your own pet store outing, remember a few necessary ground rules:
- Be certain to keep your dog securely leashed via a front-connecting harness and comfortable lead.
- Never allow your dog off-leash in busy public areas.
- Closely supervise all your Beagle's interactions with people—especially children—and other dogs.
- Make certain that your dog does not choose inappropriate toys. Your heavy chewer may pick up an item that would be dangerous to him, such as squeaky toys, small stuffed toys, or toys that are not appropriately sized or designed for him. It is your responsibility to guide him toward more appropriate Beagle-proof toys. Redirect his attention to a rope toy with tennis balls on each end or to a chew toy that will withstand his sharp teeth, such as a nontoxic durable nylon, plastic, or rubber bone or chew.

- Rope toys. These come in a variety of configurations. They are fun for your dog to chew and tend to floss his teeth at the same time. Some have balls or chew hooves on their ends, adding to the overall attraction.
- Beef shank bones. Dogs love raw bones, and these are tasty, inexpensive treats that your Beagle will love. You also can continually refill them with food treats

as another means of occupying your dog for long periods.

- Elk antlers. Another inexpensive toy that lasts forever, antlers are pure calcium, which is healthy for your dog. These don't tend to splinter or chip like some bones.
- Durable plush toys. For dogs who prefer squeaky and soft toys, tough plush toys are available. Be sure to get the type without stuffing because Beagles are aggressive chewers. Also, Beagles have a tendency to try to remove squeakers, so either remove the squeaker before giving the toy to your dog, or purchase a plush, unstuffed toy that does not contain a squeaker.

Always offer your Beagle a variety of toys, and rotate them every day or two to maintain his interest and keep his attention away from your belongings. If you offer your dog something that doesn't seem to stand up well to his heavy-duty chewing, remove and discard it. Be observant and also discard any toy if it begins to come apart or break. Small toy parts can lodge inside your Beagle's throat or intestinal tract and be hazardous to his health. For this reason, it's important to supervise your dog when giving him items to play with.

EXERCISE PEN

An exercise pen is great to have around while your Beagle is young. It will afford you greater freedom to go about your normal activities knowing that your pup is safe and secure. An exercise pen can be used indoors or out. Because it folds up for easy transport, you can also take it with you camping, visiting family and friends, or for any other activity in which you wish to include your Beagle, without endangering him or risking wearing out your welcome.

SAFETY GATES

Safety gates (baby gates) are also useful when acclimating your Beagle to your home. He is less likely to have accidents or obtain inappropriate chew toys if contained in your kitchen or another small room. Safety gates will afford him more space without full access. They are great training tools because you can easily move them, allowing more space when your dog proves that he has learned to keep his teeth on his own toys and that he can wait to relieve himself in the appropriate areas.

FEEDING YOUR BEAGLE

Beagles are notorious chow hounds. Rarely are they picky about what they eat, and they will often eat the wrong things just to investigate palatability. Puppies are especially prone to eating anything they come across, hence the need for constant vigilance when taking your Beagle pup for a walk. And no matter how hard it is to ignore those pleading big brown eyes, you must for your dog's sake.

The types of foods you choose to feed your dog should be based on sound nutritional values, not on what is least expensive on the store shelves. A good diet will maintain good health and well-being, balanced mentality, and longevity. Furthermore, controlling how much your dog eats is imperative because Beagles have a tendency to become obese as they age and slow down. Your Beagle may behave as though he is always hungry, but that doesn't mean you should feed him whenever he begs for food. A quality diet, one with a high meat content, some wholesome vegetables, and fruits, will offer him the complete and balanced nutrition that he needs for optimal vitality and development.

BALANCED CANINE DIET

Just as the Food and Drug Administration (FDA) sets a healthy food pyramid for us, there is also a set of feeding guidelines for dogs set by the American Association of Feed Control Officials (AAFCO). The AAFCO determines the protein and nutrient percentages that should be provided in a dog's daily consumption and requires dog food manufacturers to add a minimum ratio of vitamins, minerals, and enzymes to constitute appropriate and wholesome canine food products. You will not need to add additional elements to your dog's diet unless he is ill, he has a very active occupation, or you are creating his meals from scratch.

PROTEINS

Proteins are the most important nutrient and should be the main ingredient in your Beagle's diet. With the help of proteins, which are actually chains of amino acids, your Beagle's body creates 20 different amino acids that all aid in breaking down and digesting other nutrients. Dogs need proteins for energy; growth and development; maintenance and healing; help in metabolic processes; and immune system health.

The best sources of protein are from meats, particularly muscle meats. These proteins are easier for your dog to metabolize and therefore more readily available to his system. Eggs are also a good source of protein. Not all animal-based proteins are equal, however. Keratin parts, such as cow hooves, chicken feet, and chicken beaks, all contain protein, but the proteins in these animal parts are not easily utilized because the keratin surrounding them is not digestible. Many commercial foods use these parts as ingredients to add protein levels to a product, but in essence, these food manufacturers are merely adding by-product that works as filler with little nutritional value.

Grains contain proteins as well but are not as nutritious because they are not complete proteins and lack some of the essential amino acids that your Beagle requires. Corn, wheat, and soybeans are often used in commercial dog foods but act more as fillers; and sometimes, the protein contents of these ingredients also are considered in the total protein content percentages on labeling.

The AAFCO guidelines state that adult dogs should receive foods with no less than 18 percent protein. Lactating females, puppies, and dogs who have active occupations, such as military dogs, show dogs, police dogs, and sled dogs, should have a diet that consists of at least 22 percent protein.

CARBOHYDRATES AND FIBER
Your Beagle requires carbohydrates for energy. Because Beagles are active dogs who are always on the move and want to play, they utilize lots of carbohydrates in the form of glucose.

A well-balanced, nutritious diet will help your dog look and feel his best.

Carbohydrates are fed in three basic forms: cellulose, starch, and sugar. Starch and sugar are simple carbohydrates that are easily broken down into glucose and quickly digested. Samples of these include corn, wheat, rice, and oatmeal. These ingredients are added to commercial dog foods to improve their texture and bulk. However, this does not mean that they are the best carbohydrates for your Beagle to consume because dogs may have allergies to some of these ingredients, most notably corn and wheat. Healthier carbohydrates (those less likely to cause allergic reactions), such as sweet potatoes, brown rice, oatmeal, and barley, are included in many premium brands of dog foods.

The complex carbohydrate, cellulose, is often put into dog foods to add fiber and bulk, which helps the digestive system by regulating water in the large intestine, aiding in the formulation and elimination of stool. However, cellulose is more difficult to digest and is often removed from the dog's body as waste. While it contributes to bulk in the feces, few of its nutrients are actually utilized by the body, as it is merely passed through. Dogs who have sensitive digestive systems

BE AWARE!

Beware of pet food manufacturers who use grains as the main ingredient in their products and break them down into smaller components so that they can be listed separately, thereby allowing them to list a meat by-product first—even though meat makes up a smaller percentage of the total content of the food than does the grain. For example, wheat can be broken down into flour, germ meal, bran, and middlings. Because the individual percentages of each of these wheat products is less than the percentage of chicken by-product used, the manufacturer can legally place the chicken by-product ingredient first, which makes it appear that chicken is present in the greatest quantity in the food even though it is not.

Read labels carefully to prevent the purchase of a food that will not be nutritionally adequate or appropriate for your dog. Also, some grains may cause allergic reactions that result in skin irritation, loss of fur, digestive disorders, and other food-related problems, which may not appear right away. Consult your vet if you suspect that your dog is not eating properly or is having a questionable reaction to his food.

may not have a good reaction to the cellulose in their food because their systems must work harder to process it. A good substitution for cellulose would be sweet potato or pumpkin because both offer numerous nutritional advantages while also adding fiber needed by the digestive system.

There are currently no regulations regarding the amount or type of carbohydrates put into dog foods. For good nutrition, carbohydrates should not make up more than 50 percent of your dog's diet, with the majority of these being from fruits and vegetables instead of grains.

FATS

Fats are a very important part of your Beagle's diet, especially if he is an active hunting or show dog. They are an additional source of energy required by your dog because he cannot glean enough of what he needs just from proteins and carbohydrates. Fats give your Beagle a healthy coat and skin, and they are carriers of essential vitamins that can be made available only if enough fat is absorbed into the body.

The fat in dog food conveys much needed essential fatty acids, which are a huge part of keeping your Beagle healthy. Omega-3 fatty acids must be fed because dogs cannot produce them on their own. They maintain your dog's dermal layer, making his pads and nose leather flexible as well as keeping his skin supple. There are several healthy foods that offer lots of Omega-3s. These include beef, pork, and chicken. Fish oil, especially salmon oil, is another premium source. Fish oil is very helpful for dogs who have arthritis or joint injuries because the omega fatty acids aid in cartilage and synovial fluid (joint fluid) production to cushion the joints.

Like Omega-3s, Omega-6 fatty acids are another important nutrient. They help maintain a healthy coat and skin, as well as enhancing immune function. However, Omega-6s and Omega-3s should be fed at a 5 (Omega-6) to 1 (Omega-3) ratio because the two fatty acids have some opposing functions. This ratio will ensure that your dog receives all the benefits of both fatty acids. Safflower oil and corn oil are good sources of Omega-6s, while fish oil and fish meal are good sources of Omega-3s. Check with your vet to be sure your dog is receiving these fats in appropriate amounts because too much of a good thing isn't always best.

While your dog needs some healthy fat in his diet, too much can have a detrimental effect on his health. Aside from causing or aggravating certain disorders and illnesses, it can cause obesity. Beagles are prone to obesity because they love to eat and rarely control their appetite. Just as with humans, if your dog becomes too heavy, he needs to be fed a low-fat, low-carbohydrate diet until he returns to his ideal weight.

VITAMINS

Dogs require 13 essential vitamins in their daily diet that
are available to them only in the foods they eat. These
vitamins aid in the metabolic processes of the body.
They often work together with minerals and enzymes
to make nutrients available to the body's organs and
systems, thus ensuring normal digestion, reproduction,
muscle and bone growth and function, healthy skin
and hair, and blood clotting. Vitamins also assist in
the absorption and utilization of fats, proteins, and
carbohydrates. Commercial dog food manufacturers
are required to add a minimum ratio of these essential
vitamins in order to claim that their products are
completely balanced.

The type of food you feed
your dog must provide
the energy he needs to
function, as well as the
essential nutrients that
are necessary to facilitate
growth, provide energy,
and help repair the body.

There are two types of vitamins: water soluble and
fat soluble. Water-soluble vitamins cannot be stored
within your Beagle's body as can fat-soluble vitamins.
Therefore, water-soluble vitamins must be given to your
dog daily because they are continually digested and excreted.

Water-soluble vitamins include B vitamins (B1, B2, B5, B6, B7, B9, B12), choline,
and vitamin C. The B vitamins aid in growth, energy production, and intestinal
function. Pantothenic acid, or B5, is used for protein metabolism and energy
production. Folic acid, or B9, works with B12 in the body's chemical mechanisms.
Choline, a nutrient in the B complex family, is important for nervous system
function and is required for utilization of sulfur-containing amino acids. Biotin, or
B7, aids in overall enzymatic action. Vitamin C is important for the formation of
bones, teeth, and muscle tissue.

Fat-soluble vitamins include vitamins A, D, E, and K. Vitamin A is used for eye
health, bone growth, reproduction, and tissue maintenance. Vitamin D aids in the
utilization of calcium and phosphorus in bone and cartilage growth. Vitamin E is an
antioxidant that aids in muscular and reproductive function; it is often used as a
preservative in dog food. Vitamin K is required for normal blood-clotting functions.

Unlike water-soluble vitamins, fat-soluble vitamins can build up in the body and
become toxic if excess levels are stored within your dogs' fatty tissue. Be sure to
not overfeed these particular vitamins unless your veterinarian believes that your
dog is not getting enough of them in his food. Always check with your vet before
adding additional vitamin supplements to your dog's diet.

MINERALS

Minerals are divided into two groups: macro and trace minerals. Macro minerals are required in specific daily gram amounts, while trace minerals are required in milligram amounts.

Macro minerals include calcium, magnesium, phosphorus, and sulfur. Calcium is found in dairy products, poultry, and meat bones. Magnesium is found in soybeans, corn, cereal grains, and bone meals. Phosphorus and sulfur are found in meats, poultry, and fish.

Calcium aids in normal muscle, nerve, and blood function. It also activates enzymes that affect every part of every cell. This mineral is of utmost importance to your dog. Phosphorus also affects every cell, playing a large part in all the chemical reactions within your dog's body. The combination of these two minerals will strengthen your dog's bones and teeth.

Magnesium is essential for enzymatic reactions. It not only aids in bone growth and development but also promotes the absorption and metabolism of other vitamins and minerals. However, too much calcium and phosphorus can greatly impair the absorption of magnesium, so there's rarely a need to add these in supplement form to your dog's diet. The minimum standards set by AAFCO ensure that he will get sufficient amounts in his food.

As a major constituent of joint fluid and cartilage, sulfur is important in the maintenance of joint health and the synthesis of proteins. This is another ingredient that is commonly placed in dog food, but older dogs and active dogs can benefit from a little extra, which often can be found in a senior or active dog diet.

Trace minerals include iron, copper, zinc, iodine, selenium, manganese, and cobalt. Your Beagle requires only small amounts of these minerals, unless he's ill or receiving heavy exercise, in which case a supplement can be fed to replace those trace minerals that may become depleted in these circumstances.

Iron is an important trace mineral that aids in the production of red blood cells, which transport

PUPPY POINTER

Puppies need to eat more often than older dogs because they have faster metabolisms and a need for higher amounts of protein and fat. A Beagle pup under 4 months of age should be fed three times each day. Use a food specifically geared for puppies so that you can be assured that you are offering everything your Beagle needs for developing and growing normally.

oxygen to every part of the body. It is required only in small amounts, hence no need to supplement unless prescribed by your veterinarian.

Copper also aids in blood production and in the proper absorption of iron. This trace mineral plays a large part in the creation and maintenance of connective tissue. It can be found in fish, various grains, and liver. The amount of copper in commercial dog food is typically sufficient for Beagles.

Zinc helps metabolize vitamin B and aids the digestive system and overall metabolism of nutrients. It also promotes healing. Have you ever been told about taking zinc when you have a virus? That's because it aids in the healing process.

Iodine also aids in metabolism and regulates energy levels and growth. Fish is a great source of iodine.

Cobalt is a component of vitamin B12, so this trace mineral is never present without B12. Both vitamin B12 and cobalt work together to aid in the manufacture of red blood cells and to ensure healthy nervous system function.

Another trace mineral that works in conjunction with a vitamin is selenium. Selenium works with vitamin E to prevent oxidative damage to cells. It is available in most meats and cereal grains.

Manganese is a nutrient that participates in many different enzyme systems in the body. It aids in regulating nutrient metabolism and is found in whole-grain cereals and legumes. Plant-based manganese is a far better source of this trace mineral than is meat.

WATER

Water is essential for all living things. It's needed for everything the body does. It transports necessary nutrients throughout the body and carries waste materials from the system through urine and feces. It also assists digestion and regulates body temperature.

Beagles drink lots of water, so you should always make fresh water available to your dog at all times. Because water also attracts other living creatures, from microbes to insects, changing his water several times each day will ensure that your dog is less likely to ingest something that may make him ill. Providing fresh water several times a day will also prevent your Beagle from seeking out mud puddles for refreshment instead of merely as a place to splash and play.

During hot weather, your dog will drink lots more, so check and refresh water bowls frequently. Active dogs require more water as well. If you live in an area where water will freeze outdoors during the winter, using a heated bucket will ensure that your Beagle will always have something to drink. It doesn't take long for a dog to die from lack of water.

COMMERCIAL FOODS

It is far more convenient to feed your Beagle a commercial food than it is to make it yourself or to try to feed a well-balanced diet that is not readily found in a pet shop or grocery store. And, while your Beagle won't be at all picky about what he eats, you should be concerned about the type of nutrition he receives. All dogs require specific nutrients to function at their best, so choosing the right diet is important and necessary to his overall health and longevity. This includes proper brain function as well as physical function. Selecting the right foods is important for other reasons as well. Although Beagles tend to have hardy digestive systems, some ingredients may cause an allergic reaction. You'll have to do a bit of experimenting to find out what works best for your Beagle.

READING DOG FOOD LABELS

The best means of ensuring that you feed your Beagle properly is to learn how to read the labels on commercial foods. They are there for a reason. Dog food manufacturers are monitored by AAFCO, the National Research Council (NRC), and their own Pet Food Institute, a self-governing body that works with the FDA to ensure that all pet products adhere to specific guidelines. Therefore, all packaging labels are required to list ingredients, nutritional levels, and percentages of content.

Water is the most important nutrient in your dog's diet, so make sure that he has access to fresh, cool water at all times.

The best means of ensuring that you feed your Beagle properly is to learn how to read the labels on commercial foods, which tell you how much protein, fat, fiber, and moisture is contained in each product.

First, learn to recognize the product's identity, which appears on the label near the name of the product. This will generally tell you the overall availability of meat proteins it contains. For example, a beef-based product can be labeled Beef for Dogs, which is required to be 95 percent beef; or Beef Dog Food, which is required to be at least 70 percent beef; or Beef Dinner, Beef Entrée, or Beef Platter, which is required to be at least 23 percent beef. The types you should avoid are those labeled Dog Food With Beef or Beef-Flavored, which may consist of less than 3 percent actual meat.

The information panel on the packaging informs you of how much protein, fat, fiber, and moisture is contained in the food. This is an analysis of the food nutrients, which will help you determine whether it is the right food for your Beagle. Keep in mind that a more active dog or one who is caring for pups will need higher levels of protein and fat, as mentioned earlier.

The ingredient list displays what is in the food in descending order, based on the amount contained on a dry-weight basis. Essentially, the first three items listed comprise the majority of the ingredients. Therefore, if meat is listed as the first few ingredients, you can be reasonably assured that it is a healthy food. Seeing corn, corn meal, wheat, meat by-products, or meat meal listed at the top of the list indicates a food of lesser quality—one from which your dog will be unable to extract the essential proteins and nutrients needed for good digestion and energy production.

Dog food companies change ownership fairly frequently. It is helpful to hang onto a list of ingredients and to periodically check the bags and cans you purchase to ensure that nothing changes.

Label Terminology

Understanding label terminology is also helpful in determining whether you are purchasing a well-balanced, quality food product. Here are a few terms you should know:

- By-products: These are nonhuman-grade proteins derived from animal carcasses that vary greatly in digestibility. There's really no means of knowing whether or not they will be helpful to your dog. However, if an ingredient is of nonhuman grade, it is best to steer clear of it in general.
- Meat and bone meal: This is processed tissue and bone, which is often a good source of protein.
- Animal by-product meal: These are ingredients used for filler. Pet food manufacturers can claim their protein levels, but rarely are any of these proteins digestible. These ingredients include hooves, hide trimmings, manure, beaks, feet, horns, and sometimes intestinal contents. Would you really want to feed this to your Beagle?
- Meat by-products: These are actually healthy ingredients because they comprise organ meat (high in amino acids), blood, bones, fat, and intestines—all ingredients that aid in maintaining appropriate protein and fat levels.
- Meat meal: This is meal made from processed animal tissues. It is a great source of protein and does not contain more than 14 percent indigestible materials.
- Poultry by-products: This includes nonrendered clean parts of carcasses of slaughtered poultry, such as heads, feet, and viscera, which are not a good source of protein.
- Poultry by-product meal: This meal consists of the ground, rendered, clean parts of the carcasses of slaughtered poultry, such as necks, feet, undeveloped eggs, and intestines, but exclusive of feathers except in such amounts as might occur unavoidably in good processing practices. It is not a good source of protein and, once ingested, will likely be excreted by your dog.

DRY DOG FOODS

There are many benefits to feeding dry dog food. Prominent among the reasons are that it's easy to store and easy to feed. Beagles thrive on dry food as the major portion of their diets, provided it is of sufficient quality to provide all the nutrients required by an active breed.

Other advantages include maintaining your dog's dental health because the hard pieces massage the gums and scrape the teeth clear of tartar. Dry foods also do not spoil as readily as other types of food. You can store them in a clean, dark location for up to four months, and they will continue retaining their nutritional value.

If your Beagle were given the choice between dry or canned food, he would choose canned food because it is more odiferous and flavorful. Beagles are rarely picky, however, and will often do well with dry kibble, provided you add some fresh meats, fruits, and vegetables now and then.

CANNED FOODS

Though more expensive than dry food, canned food is also more nutritious and less processed than dry food. It is easy to store, until opened. If you don't use the entire contents of the can, the food must be refrigerated; even then, it will not maintain freshness for more than a couple days.

Because canned dog food is less processed, the manufacturer rarely has to include preservatives or fillers. The food contains a high portion of whole, unprocessed ingredients, making it far more nutritious.

Canned food also contains more moisture than dry food. Because dogs obtain a good portion of moisture from their food, it is a good idea to add some canned food to your dog's meals. This will enhance his nutrition and ensure that he eats everything quickly.

SEMI-MOIST FOODS

Your Beagle will scarf this up like a treat. In fact, many treats are merely semi-moist dog food. Just keep in mind that in order to preserve foods in this manner, the manufacturer must add sugar and starch as well as preservatives. In small quantities, this won't amount to much; but in large quantities, the excess sugar can be detrimental to your Beagle's health. In fact, some of the preservatives used have been proven to harm a dog's liver. Do not feed semi-moist foods in large amounts and certainly not as your dog's main meals.

NONCOMMERCIAL FOODS

There's another way to ensure that your Beagle receives a good diet without relying on a commercial product: You can make it yourself.

Although canines are omnivorous, meat is required as the main portion of their diets. Keeping this in mind, you can prepare some great foods for your dog right in your own kitchen. However, make certain that you carefully research nutrient levels to ensure that you are providing your Beagle with the nutritionally complete and balanced diet he needs to be fed every day to remain healthy.

HOME-COOKED DIETS

Cooking for your dog is a great way to provide him with quality care, as long as you have the time to shop for, prepare, and cook fresh ingredients. A home-cooked diet does not imply just throwing leftovers into his bowl. As discussed, dogs need a carefully planned diet that contains specific ingredients in order to thrive. The following is a basic recipe for a home-cooked meal. You can mix it up by changing the meat sources and vegetables, but be certain to add the appropriate vitamin, mineral, and fat supplements needed to ensure that his body continues to function at premium levels.

First, cook some meat. This can be poultry, red meat, pork, or lamb. Make certain to cook it thoroughly, until there's no red (uncooked) meat inside. This will prevent any chance of bacterial contamination. Next, grind up some vegetables, such as broccoli, carrots, or green beans. To add roughage and vitamins, add some cooked brown rice. Add some fish oil to ensure that your dog receives the appropriate levels of fatty acids.

When you have the time to create this concoction, make enough to last a week or two so that you can more easily manage to consistently feed your Beagle in this manner.

Dogs require a period of a week or two to acclimate to a new diet, so you don't want to suddenly switch your dog to a commercial food when he is used to eating your home cooking or vice versa.

RAW DIETS

This type of diet was all the rage a while ago. It was considered a great means of ensuring that dogs received appropriate nutrients because processed commercial food was thought to lose many essential nutrients during its manufacture. However, it is mandatory for commercial pet food to have a minimum amount of specific nutrients in order to be considered completely balanced. Hence, feeding a raw diet is merely a preference and comes with many additional considerations.

First of all, bacteria can be present in raw food. You will need to store the food and prepare it carefully in order to prevent making your Beagle ill. Not only can salmonella and botulism be fatal to dogs, but it also is very much so to humans.

A raw diet requires much more of your time commitment than a home-cooked meal does. Prior to feeding the meat, it will need to be soaked for hours in a bacteria-killing substance, such as grapefruit seed extract. All vegetables will need to be blended in order to break down the cellulose that encases the nutrients within them. The grains used, such as brown rice, will also need to be cooked, just as in regular home-made meals. You will need to be certain to feed your dog some hard substances to aid in his dental health. Real bones are great for this, as are carrots. When feeding a raw diet, be certain to rotate the muscle and organ meat because your Beagle will need the nutrients from both.

It is safest to freeze a raw diet when storing it in order to prevent bacterial growth. Several commercial manufacturers now offer raw diets, making this type of feeding a little easier on you. All you have to do is purchase it, keep it frozen until use, microwave it, and feed it.

NOTHING IN LIFE SHOULD BE FREE

Dogs like to have occupations. Beagles were bred to hunt, working for their food. If food were available to them at all times, they would not exercise at all and just eat all the time. This, of course, creates an obesity problem. If your dog is an urban or suburban companion who does not spend time in the field hunting, the problem of gaining excess weight may be even more of a concern.

To ensure that your Beagle maintains a healthy body and remains mentally willing to work for you if he engages in hunting or sporting activities, he should not be offered food freely. Free feeding can cause obesity and will also make it difficult to maintain housetraining schedules, especially when your Beagle is young. By feeding scheduled meals, you can get him onto a regular relief schedule and know exactly how much food he is consuming.

HOW MUCH TO FEED

The amounts you feed depend largely on the age and exercise level of the individual dog. Puppies generally need twice the amount of food as adult dogs because they have a faster metabolism and are very active. Senior dogs tend to sleep much of the time, therefore requiring fewer calories. As a general rule, while a pup might eat 1 cup of good-quality, high-protein food three times each day, a spayed or neutered adult might need only 2/3 to 1 cup twice each day and a senior dog 1/2 to 2/3 cup twice each day. The best means of knowing is to look at your dog's body, specifically his abdomen where his rib cage ends and in front of his hip bones. While Beagles are generally well-rounded, your dog should still have a noticeable waistline.

Also keep in mind that the nutritional needs of your Beagle will change depending on his age. Puppies need more fats and complex carbohydrates

Dog Tale

I recently met a 2-year-old Beagle named Gus. He had spent the past year living in a small apartment with his owner. Without being able to get much exercise, he had put on a lot of weight. In fact, he was so heavy that he had trouble breathing. Moreover, his coat was very dry and his foot pads were cracked. After asking about his diet, I discovered that he was getting free fed a dry food high in carbohydrates and by-products. It was the worst possible scenario for a sedate adult Beagle.

Consulting with his owner, I suggested how to achieve healthy weight loss through sufficient daily exercise and better food choices. Gus's diet was changed to one low in carbohydrates and starches (to reduce unhealthy calories) and higher in protein and amino acids (to gloss up his coat and make his skin more supple). Rather than free feeding, he received two scheduled meals per day. As a way to make him feel full, his dry food intake was reduced to a half-cup twice each day, along with some canned green beans and pumpkin to give him fiber without the added calories. He did not need much more food than that because he never had a chance to run freely outdoors. The majority of his exercise was on leash.

I saw Gus again a month later. He still lived in a small apartment, but his coat was shiny and soft. I actually saw the start of a waistline as well. The best part was that he could run around for a while and play with the other dogs without getting tired as easily. Overall, Gus had become a happier, healthier dog, looking more like a 2 year old than an ill 12 year old.

than adults, and seniors need more fiber and fewer carbohydrates. Adult dogs generally do well with a high-protein diet, provided they get a lot of exercise.

WHEN TO FEED

Your dog should be offered his meals twice each day, morning and evening, and earn any treats and other rewards by performing something for you, such as a sit or come. Sitting before being given his meals is a great way to gain control of him and create positive associations with good behavior. Teaching your Beagle to earn his rewards will keep him wanting to perform for you instead of becoming a couch potato. An active Beagle must exercise both his brain and body, ensuring a longer, healthier life and a better relationship with you.

GROOMING YOUR BEAGLE

Beagles are wash-and-wear dogs, so taking care of their grooming needs is fairly easy. Basically, they require regular brushing and an occasional bath because they are an active breed and are prone to rolling in smelly things when playing outdoors. And, as with any dog, they need to have their nails trimmed, ears cleaned, and teeth maintained regularly to remain healthy.

Beagles love attention, and grooming is a great means of spending quality time with your canine companion while also ensuring his well-being. As you groom your dog, you can look for signs of parasites and examine his overall condition with a full-body check. Making grooming a regular part of your dog's daily activities is a good routine to establish. Besides, a clean doggy is happier because he will earn more hugs and kisses from his humans. What better reward can a Beagle ask for?

Along with keeping your Beagle looking and feeling his best, a frequent hands-on exam is a first line of defense against illness. When grooming your Beagle, ensure that all his parts are in good working order. Have a look at his teeth, ears, and foot pads. His teeth should be pearly white, with healthy pink gums. His ears should be clean and not have any odor. His foot pads should be soft and pliable, without cracks or scrapes. He should have a shiny coat and smooth skin. This begins with a good diet, but it also depends on good grooming. When you brush or massage with a grooming glove, you are releasing skin oils that help to keep the coat shiny.

Beagles have a close, hard, medium coat, so taking care of their grooming needs is fairly easy.

GROOMING SUPPLIES

Although your Beagle is easy to keep clean, you will still require some basic grooming supplies to help you get the job done:

- Grooming glove: Beagles have short fur, so a grooming glove will serve better at removing dead fur and massaging the skin than will a hard-bristle brush.
- Soft-bristle brush: A soft-bristle brush will be needed for grooming the face and ears and for pulling off loose fur and dirt.
- Flea comb: A flea comb is used to remove parasites.
- Nail clippers: Clippers are required to do a proper pedicure, which should be done every four to six weeks.
- Canine toothbrush and toothpaste: Along with flavored, nonenzyme toothpaste, a three-sided brush makes dental maintenance easier because it allows you to clean all surfaces at the same time.

Other items that are good to have on hand are:

- Styptic powder: Styptic powder can stem the flow of blood in case you accidentally trim a nail too close to the quick.
- Cotton balls: Cotton balls are soft and safe for cleaning the ears and around the eyes and nose.
- Canine shampoo and conditioner: Canine shampoos and conditioners are made specifically for your dog's skin and coat; human shampoos are too harsh and can strip necessary natural oils out of dog hair. Your dog may be bathed every few weeks, or as needed.
- Herbal ear cleaner or mineral oil: It's best to use pet products made specifically for this purpose, although some vets recommend using mineral oil.
- Absorbent towels: Several towels will be needed to dry your dog's coat after a bath, as well as to keep him from getting chilled.

COAT AND SKIN CARE

While a Beagle's grooming needs are basic, his coat can become dull and coarse and his skin dry and irritated without proper care. To keep your dog's skin and coat in tip-top condition, he requires frequent brushing and a bath whenever necessary, along with a routine all-over body check.

BRUSHING

During the cooler months of the year, brushing twice each week is sufficient. In the warmer months, however, you should brush your dog daily in order to discover any parasites that might be lurking in his coat.

Always begin by bringing up loose and dead fur. This is done using a grooming glove, which has little nubs that both massage your dog's skin and bring loose fur to the surface.

Starting at the back of the head, use a circular motion down the head and around the neck. Then move down the shoulders, along the back, and down the sides. To ensure that you cover the entire abdomen, be methodical. Once the main body is complete, do the tail to the tip, and follow with the legs and feet. And, most of all, don't forget the tummy. That'll be the favorite spot!

Once the hair has been loosened with the grooming glove, use a soft-bristle brush on the coat. First brush the face, being careful to not go too near the eyes, especially if your Beagle is still wiggly. Work your way down the body, with short scooping motions to get up loose hair. Every so often, clean out the brush by scraping it along a grooming glove and shaking the glove out over a trash can. This will ensure that you are not redistributing the fur back onto your dog. Always begin at the top of your dog's head and work your way down to the feet.

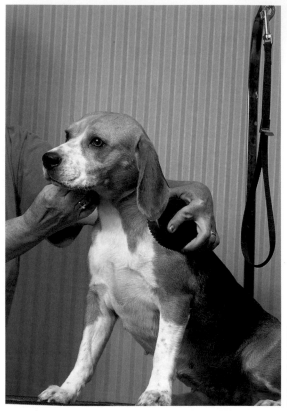

Brushing helps to loosen and remove dead hair and debris and stimulates the natural oils that keep your Beagle's skin and coat in top condition.

BATHING

Because your Beagle loves the outdoors and has a natural hunting ability, it is highly likely that you will need to bathe him regularly—every two to four weeks and maybe even more often, depending on how much he likes to roll in stinky things. Aside from removing dirt and debris and making him smell better, bathing will also help remove dead fur, control external parasites, and allow you to better examine him because you will see his skin surface better when he is wet.

Bath Training

Before you actually bathe your Beagle, you will need to teach him tub manners.

To acclimate him to bathing, place him inside the dry tub and offer him some treats or a toy. Play with him by wiggling a toy in his mouth or playing fetch in the tub. You can also place some treats in the tub so that he can search for them, like a treasure hunt game. This will make the experience of being in the tub happy and rewarding. Praise him for behaving and being calm. Do this training exercise every day for a week. It is likely that by then, he will be trying to get into the tub before you lift him into it.

Next, run some shallow water into the tub. Beagles generally have no fear of water. In fact, it might add to the fun, like playing in a big puddle. Repeat the rewards and praise as before. You obviously can't place treats into the tub now, but when he begins to look around for them, you can reward him for behaving well and offer a treat by hand.

Be sure to offer lots of praise and rewards throughout the process to keep it a positive experience. Once your Beagle is comfortable being in the water, you can begin to give him a full bath.

Getting Ready for the Bath

Prepare the tub by placing a nonskid rubber mat onto the bottom. Have all bathing apparatus ready: canine shampoo and conditioner, cotton balls, absorbent towels, etc. If you do not have a spray hose, you should have a large plastic cup on hand for thoroughly rinsing your dog's coat.

Before starting the bath, place some cotton balls into your Beagle's ears to prevent water from getting inside of them. Moisture that remains in the ear canal can cause an ear infection, and large droopy ears do not often dry out completely.

How to Bathe Your Dog

If your Beagle is still skittish about being bathed, you can help him to adjust to the routine by taking things slowly and reinforcing each step he takes toward behaving in the tub. Eventually, he may even enjoy having a bath.

Begin by placing your dog into the tub before turning on the water. As you run the water, give him treats and praise to keep him enthusiastic about the experience. Make certain the water is not gushing out of the faucet and that it is a comfortable temperature for him. Keep in mind that a dog's normal body temperature is 101°F (38°C), so you do not want the water to be hot; it should be warm and slightly above room temperature. Do not fill the tub more than a few inches (a few cm).

Continue to reward your dog as you gently pour water over him or wet him down with a spray hose. Never spray your dog's face, which will frighten him; instead, clean his face with a dampened washcloth. Once your dog's coat is completely wet, you can pour some doggy shampoo onto your hands and rub them together a little to distribute the shampoo evenly on your palms. Then massage the shampoo onto your dog's coat, starting with the top of his head and working your way down his body, just as you did when using the grooming glove. Rinse him thoroughly so that no soap remains in his coat. Repeat this process when applying conditioner. Or you can use a spray on, leave-in conditioner, which is far easier because it doesn't need to be rinsed out.

Once your dog is thoroughly rinsed, dry him with some warm fluffy towels. Take the cotton out of his ears, and make certain to pat his outer ears dry. It would be a good idea to keep him indoors until he dries, or he might do what comes naturally and roll in the dirt to dry off.

For the first few baths, you will want to reinforce good behavior with treats and praise, especially during rinsing, which makes some dogs uncomfortable. It's difficult to thoroughly remove all the shampoo and conditioner from the coat if your wiggly pup is constantly biting at your hands and trying to escape. The bathing ritual will be much more enjoyable once your Beagle chooses to calmly remain in the tub until the job is finished.

BEAGLE

As your dog acclimates to the bathing process, gradually require his good behavior a little longer before rewarding him. You will eventually be able to phase out the treats and reward his good behavior using only praise.

DENTAL CARE

Your dog can suffer from plaque, tartar build up, and gingivitis as easily as most humans can. Because your dog cannot take care of his dental needs by himself, it is up to you to do so. Brushing at least twice each week will ensure that he has healthy teeth and gums well into his senior years. Good oral hygiene also helps keep the body healthy because the ability to tear and chew is the first part of the digestive process. Additionally, gum disease can cause infection that can travel to your Beagle's organs, thus affecting his general health.

Frequent and thorough brushing is essential. And applying toothpaste that is meat flavored will give your Beagle a positive association with having his teeth cleaned. Unlike products made for humans, canine toothpaste is edible and infused with inviting flavor and aroma.

HOW TO BRUSH THE TEETH

Begin by first allowing your dog to sniff the toothbrush and lick off some toothpaste. He will learn to identify the toothbrush with a tasty treat. Once your dog likes the idea of the toothbrush, lift one of his lips and brush his teeth in an up and down motion for just a couple seconds. Allow your dog to lick his teeth and gums. It's highly likely that he will want more.

Gradually increase the amount of time you work on your dog's teeth. You will know his comfort level by his behavior. If he begins to fuss, stop and wait a few minutes before trying again. All new activities should be performed in small increments, allowing your dog to adjust and accept the process without having to be forced into complying. Be sure to clean his teeth all the way around. The top teeth are the most important, however, because they often help keep the bottom ones clean.

Once your dog is accustomed to this routine, brush regularly.

EAR CARE

Beagles have long, folded-over ears that cover the ear canals. Even when they move or "perk" their ears to capture sounds, their ear flaps do not lift. Long ears limit adequate air circulation, which allows moisture to build up in the ear, creating a warm, moist environment for bacterial infection; and repeated infections may cause loss of hearing. Debris and earwax will often collect inside the ear canal. For these reasons, you need to pay special attention to the health of your dog's ears.

Your Beagle should have his ears cleaned at least once each week with a good herbal antiseptic cleaner to keep his inner ears healthy and smelling good.

HOW TO CLEAN THE EARS

First, teach your Beagle to hold still for ear cleaning by gradually introducing him to the process and rewarding him for good behavior, just as you did for brushing and bathing. Teaching your dog to hold still while you groom him will prevent you from injuring him, especially in delicate areas like the ears and eyes.

Once your dog will hold still for even a short period, put a few drops of herbal ear cleaner into the ear canal. Then, gently massage the base of the ear canal for about 30 seconds to loosen any debris. Next, take a clean cotton ball soaked in herbal ear cleaner (or mineral oil) and wipe around the opening of the ear canal, then the crevices and outer ear on the underside of the ear flap. Never force a cotton ball into the ear canal; clean only the outer ear surfaces. Even a small piece of cotton left inside the ear canal can cause problems, along with likely pushing ear wax and dirt against the eardrum.

EYE CARE

Beagles love to romp in the yard or woods and roll in the dirt. With all this outdoor activity, they are likely to get dirt granules or other debris in their eyes. Their eyes can easily become scratched as well. Squinting may indicate an abrasion or that debris may be trapped under the eyelid. If the whites of the eyes become red or develop a little bit of yellow discharge, it may indicate allergies or an infection. To be safe, consult your veterinarian.

HOW TO CLEAN THE EYES

Using a warm, wet washcloth, gently wipe away any discharge that has gathered in the corners of the eye. Carefully wipe around the eye, never directly on the eye's surface. If there is dirt or debris inside the eye, flush it out with a canine sterile eye wash. These are available at pet stores.

NAIL CARE

Your dog will need to have his nails trimmed every six weeks at the very least. While you can always take him to a veterinarian or groomer to have this done, it would be less stressful and less expensive to learn how to do this properly yourself. Your Beagle will have full trust in you because the two of you have bonded and learned how to communicate with each other.

Basic foot care keeps your dog's feet healthy. Your Beagle will need to have his nails trimmed about every six weeks.

HOW TO TRIM THE NAILS

Begin by having your dog sit or lie down (see Chapter 7: Training Your Beagle). Once he's in place, take a front paw and hold it close to the toes. You will see that the nails curve to a point. Within the nails are nerve endings and blood vessels. If the nails are clear or white, you will easily see these. If the nails are black, however, you won't see them and must estimate how much to trim. If your dog allows you to hold his foot and remains calm during this examination, reward his good behavior by giving him a treat. Gently handle and massage all four feet, offering a small treat now and then to help him associate nail grooming

Dog Tale

Senior dogs benefit greatly from regular grooming. As dogs age, they find it increasingly more difficult to groom themselves, but just as with humans, they still like to feel clean and comfortable. Regular grooming will also help you keep track of your senior's overall condition, letting you know immediately of changes that can be detrimental to his health.

As your Beagle gets older and arthritis sets in, he will not appreciate being lifted into the tub or may not even have the patience for bathing. I made my senior more comfortable by using dog wipes that I purchased at the pet supply store. They worked well to clean him sufficiently while also removing loose hair and dirt. He was able to rest on his side as I groomed him. Afterward, I'd reward him with a gentle massage to soothe his achy joints and muscles. Spot cleaning with wipes is especially useful for dogs who experience incontinence or bowel problems, which is common with certain internal health issues, or when dogs forget housetraining skills as a result of canine cognitive dysfunction.

with something pleasant.

Once your dog remains calm while having his feet handled, try clipping a nail or two, again offering a small treat every so often. Nip off only the very end with nail clippers. An emery board or dremel tool will help smooth the rough edges off the nail. Keep in mind that trimming only the very end of the nails will require that you trim more frequently, but doing so will make it less likely that you'll cut into a blood vessel, also called the quick. Cutting the quick not only is painful to your dog but causes profuse bleeding; hence the need to have styptic powder nearby to stem the flow of blood. Your dog will be hesitant to sit calmly through nail-trimming sessions if this happens once too often.

Try trimming a few more nails each time you groom your dog's feet. As he becomes more comfortable with this entire process, gradually make him remain in place a bit longer between receiving each reward. Then alternate between a treat and verbal praise. In time, you can substitute treats with praise.

At first, nail-trimming sessions might be intense for both of you. It is sometimes helpful to attempt to trim the nails when your Beagle is sleepy and relaxed. He'll be less likely to have the energy to protest the situation. Take frequent breaks to allow your dog a chance to rest and relax. Keep the experience positive by offering lots of praise, remaining calm, and rewarding him often.

FINDING A PROFESSIONAL GROOMER

Although you will not have to take your Beagle to a professional groomer very often, you should become familiar with one who is conveniently located near your home and whom you can trust with your dog. While you can attend to most of your dog's needs yourself, there may be some chores you are uncomfortable with. For example, if your Beagle tends to get impacted anal glands, a groomer can excise them as easily as a veterinarian can and give your dog a spa treatment at the same time. You will pick up your clean-smelling and huggable dog without having to do anything other than a bit of homework prior to your dog's visit to check the qualifications of the groomer and the quality of the services offered at his shop.

Finding a good groomer is as important as finding a good vet. Checking a shop's website on the Internet will inform you of the groomer's credentials, but an in-person inspection will give you an opportunity to see first-hand how the dogs are handled, as well as allow you to inspect the premises, especially for cleanliness.

You also can find a reliable groomer by asking your veterinarian, who may be able to recommend someone in your area. Speak with other dog owners, too. They likely have met and utilize the services of someone they trust. If you board your dog, it is highly likely that the facility offers grooming services. This is a great place to have your dog groomed because they are already familiar with him, so he will likely feel more comfortable being in their hands.

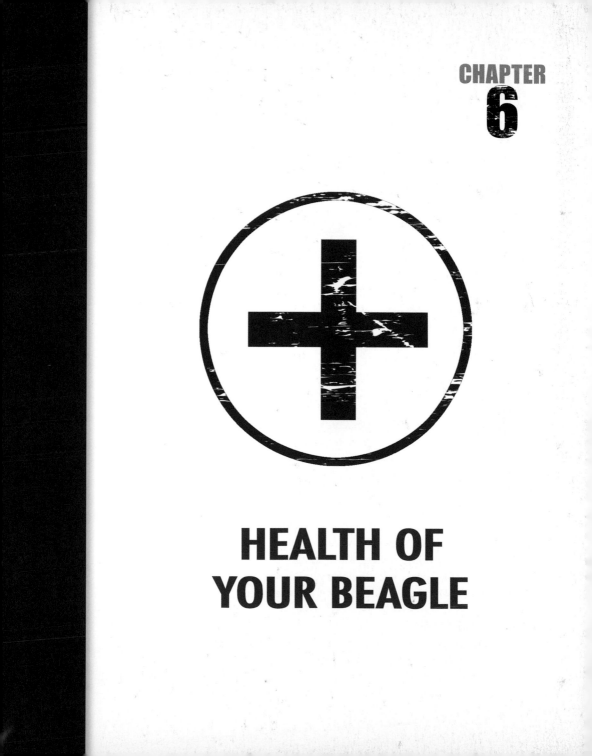

HEALTH OF
YOUR BEAGLE

Beagles are very hardy hounds but still require regular veterinary care just like any other breed of dog. All dogs must have specific vaccinations, an annual exam, regular deworming, preventive care, and medical treatments from time to time, especially as they age. Just as you would carefully choose your own doctor, you will need to put in a little research to ensure that you choose the right veterinarian for your canine companion.

FINDING A VETERINARIAN

While proximity to your veterinarian is a great convenience, this does not always mean a good match. There are a great variety of veterinary disciplines: traditional medicine, alternative medicine, and progressive veterinary medicine. Your locale may play a large part in what your options are. If you live in an urban or suburban area, you are likely to have more choices than if you live in a rural area, where the majority of the veterinarians practice traditional medicine.

Also keep in mind that you do not have to use just one veterinarian for all your dog's care. Many have become specialized, just as in human medicine, and are more capable of addressing specific ailments than a general practitioner is. For example, there are veterinary ophthalmologists, cardiologists, orthopedic surgeons, neurologists, and much more.

Your first step is to speak with friends and neighbors who have dogs. Most likely, they use the services of a local veterinarian and can relate their experiences. If you purchased your Beagle from a breeder, she may have a list of veterinarians whom she recommends. If you adopted your dog, you might have access to the veterinarian who worked closely with the adoption agency. Many veterinarians offer their services to rescue groups and humane societies at a greatly discounted rate. Although providing this service is of great benefit to both the organization and to your initial investment, it does not always mean that this veterinarian will perfectly fit all your dog's needs, but it is a great place to start.

While searching for a veterinarian whose qualifications meet your criteria as well as your dog's individual needs, also consider the differences between taking him to a veterinary clinic versus a single veterinarian. There are pros and cons to each situation, which will affect your overall experience.

SINGLE-VET CLINICS

The advantages of having a veterinarian who works alone are the more personable service and the individual recognition that goes along with this type of veterinary practice. Knowing all her clients personally, she does not have to consult with other veterinarians regarding your pet's medical history.

However, if she takes on more clients than she can handle, her time with your dog will be shorter. She may not offer emergency hours, and you may be referred to an emergency veterinary clinic during weekends, evenings, and holidays. These vets are commonly general practitioners, referring out unique cases to specialists who may be a long distance away.

MULTI-VET CLINICS

The advantages of having several veterinarians available are numerous. First of all, one is likely to be available to handle emergencies. Also, if your dog has abnormal symptoms that are not easily diagnosed, the veterinary group can brainstorm together to discuss how to best treat the problem. Furthermore, one of the veterinarians is likely to have a specialty, such as alternative or holistic methodologies, offering you more treatment options.

Once you decide to welcome a Beagle into your home, one of your first priorities is to find the best possible veterinarian for him.

CHECKLIST OF REQUIREMENTS

Regardless of which type of clinic you choose, be sure to use a checklist of requirements to ensure that you will be comfortable having your Beagle treated at the facility.

The Veterinarian

First and foremost, you want to be confident of your veterinarian's credentials and level of experience, in particular with Beagles. You also want to ensure that both you and your dog have a good rapport with her.

If you are lucky, you can find a veterinarian who is educated in behavior and nutrition. Nutrition is a very important factor affecting the overall well-being of your Beagle. And, because behavior changes can often foretell physical maladies, a veterinarian who can distinguish between these types of abnormalities and those caused by nonmedical issues can often treat the problem before symptoms advance.

Asking the veterinarian questions during your first visit will give you a better idea if this is the best fit for you and your Beagle. For example, ask which vaccinations are recommended, why, and how often they should be given. A traditional veterinarian will suggest yearly vaccinations unless otherwise indicated. However, a veterinarian who understands the viability of regular early vaccinations will also offer to do a titer test, which will ensure that your Beagle remains safe and sufficiently inoculated without over-burdening his system, which can lead to allergic reactions.

Ask whether the veterinarian offers alternative or holistic treatment approaches. A holistic veterinarian considers the entire dog—both his physical and emotional wellness—not just his symptoms. There may be a simple cause for a symptom that can be cured by changing the dog's diet or routine, or an approach to treatment that a traditional veterinarian may miss due to lack of experience in these areas. For example, a holistic veterinarian may use herbal or homeopathic products that help the body develop antibodies to heal itself. Or a veterinarian knowledgeable in alternative medicine might suggest acupuncture as a means of treating pain instead of conventional medication, thereby reducing the possibility of side effects.

Ask the veterinarian about her policies regarding emergency and specialty treatments. Does she offer these services, or can she direct you to another doctor who does? Veterinarians often associate with regional emergency and specialty clinics. When asked, she should be able to provide you with a list and contact information.

When you take your Beagle to a veterinarian for appropriate health treatment and prevention, you may have questions regarding specific procedures and care. Your vet should take her time with you and answer everything thoroughly, making certain that you are satisfied and that your Beagle will thrive in every respect. She should also be up front about the costs of treatment and all care options and their possible results. These should be explained clearly and patiently so that you have a complete understanding and can make an educated decision about what is best for your Beagle.

The American Animal Hospital Association (AAHA) provides a list of associated veterinarians by city and state. You can access this information via their website www.aahanet.org. Most veterinarians are members and adhere to their specific guidelines.

The Clinic

When choosing a veterinarian for your Beagle, you also want to make sure the clinic meets acceptable standards. The entire facility should be clean and smell good. Beagles have a much better sense of smell than we do, and you can be sure that if he smells fear, waste, or heavy cleaners, he won't be happy and relaxed.

Efficient record keeping is also essential. Your veterinarian should have individual files for each pet and/or a computer record easily available. As human medical doctors are switching to electronic record keeping, so should veterinarians be, as this offers a more efficient means of maintaining accurate information, including X-rays and other test records.

When taking your dog to the vet, you also want to enjoy your visit. This can happen only if the facility has a friendly and courteous staff. All it takes is one incompetent or unpleasant person to spoil the experience and make you and your pet feel insecure. And you can be sure that your Beagle will sense whether or not you are happy.

CHECKUPS: THE YEARLY BEAGLE BUGLE CALL

It is vital that your Beagle gets an annual physical exam. Not only will he receive the vaccinations he requires, but your veterinarian will also do a thorough health check to ensure that everything is in good working order. This examination fills you in on your Beagle's current health status.

Your veterinarian will listen to your dog's heart and lungs. An anomaly in the heart's normal rhythm can be the symptom of something requiring immediate attention, such as heartworm or kennel cough. If there's a heart murmur, your veterinarian can make note of it and keep track of it to make sure it does not worsen over time. If there is an irregularity in the sound of the lungs, she can order further testing to identify the cause.

A thorough examination of your Beagle's eyes, ears, and nose can show signs of infection or parasite infestation, even if no other symptoms are noticeable. A discharge from the eyes or nose can be a sign of contagion, such as bordetellosis or parvovirus. Ears can harbor infections or mites, both of which can become destructive to your Beagle's well-being if not treated right away.

A dog's skin and coat also shout out when something might be going on. Your veterinarian will do a close examination, searching for hot spots or raw areas, as well as external parasites such as fleas and ticks. External parasites leave distinct traces because they lay eggs or cause scabs from bites. You can use regular topical parasite control, but your dog may still be bitten and suffer an allergic reaction.

An abdominal examination is done to feel for lumps or sensitive areas that might have been injured or may be harboring a tumor. As dogs age, they tend to develop fatty deposits just under the skin. Your veterinarian will keep track of these, checking for firmness or changes that indicate the presence of a problem. Soreness along the spine also can indicate a physical malady that should be addressed immediately in order to prevent further injury.

To help your Beagle remain relaxed during his exam, feed him a few yummy treats to keep his mind off of it and to associate the visit with something positive. This will also help your veterinarian because keeping your dog relatively still during the procedure means she can complete it more efficiently. Just don't offer the treats when the veterinarian is using her stethoscope. The sounds of munching can be quite loud, preventing her from hearing the heart and lung functions.

VACCINATIONS

While not all veterinarians agree on vaccination schedules for adult dogs, they do agree on vaccination schedules for puppies. Your Beagle should receive his first vaccinations at 8 weeks of age. These will be for distemper, hepatitis, leptospirosis, parvovirus, and parainfluenza (DHLPP). The second set of vaccinations and preventives will be for deworming; the first deworming should be done at 5 weeks of age because many pups inherit roundworm from their mother.

The DHLPP vaccine is administered in three parts, with each booster administered two weeks apart. When your Beagle pup is at least 3 months of age, he can receive a rabies vaccination, which will be administered again in a year and then every three years thereafter.

In the past, adult dogs received DHLPP boosters yearly, but recent studies have shown that the vaccine remains effective longer, especially if the dog has been receiving regular boosters for a few years. A titer test (blood test) can show the current efficacy of the remaining serum in the dog's system. Because some dogs can have a reaction to being over-vaccinated, doing a titer is far safer, especially as your Beagle ages.

There are a few other optional vaccines available, and you should consider discussing the need for these with your vet, especially if you will be exposing your Beagle to other dogs on a regular basis, such as at doggy daycare, at an overnight boarding facility, or at a dog park.

CORE VACCINES

Core vaccines are considered most important and are administered to help prevent diseases for which there is no real treatment except relief of symptoms until the disease has run its course. Sometimes an antibiotic may be given to support the dog's immune system if it is severely compromised by the disease.

Canine Parvovirus

A highly contagious virus affecting dogs, parvovirus kills the cells of the small intestine, making it difficult for dogs to absorb intestinal fluids. Symptoms include bloody diarrhea, vomiting, and a bad odor. A mild infection can often be treated, providing recovery in a few days; however, a severe infection can be fatal, especially in puppies.

Because puppies are highly susceptible to parvovirus, it is the first inoculation they receive, with two booster vaccines given two weeks apart. During this time, a pup is only partially immune and should be kept away from dogs with whom you are unfamiliar.

Distemper

Distemper is very common in feral pets and wild animals. It is caused by a virus that attacks the lymph nodes, killing all the major cells that normally defend the body against invading viruses. An infected animal becomes immune suppressed and thus is at risk for contracting other diseases as well.

The most common symptoms of distemper are an ocular discharge and fever. However, the symptoms can vary and include coughing, weight loss, diarrhea, and lack of appetite. Most puppies who contract the disease die, while older dogs who have a stronger immune system have a 50 percent chance of survival, though often with severe debilitation that may include seizures, lameness, and blindness.

Vaccinations help protect a dog against disease.

The distemper vaccine is given as part of the DHLPP series. Your Beagle should receive a yearly booster, though after 3 years of age a titer test can determine whether the body maintains enough anti-viral serum to make a booster unnecessary at that time.

Hepatitis

Hepatitis is an acute infection of the liver caused by canine adenovirus type-1 (CAV-1). Although not as common as parvovirus and distemper, hepatitis can be fatal if left untreated and secondary liver disease can develop. Unfortunately, it is not easily recognizable because the symptoms are generally fever and lethargy, which can be mistaken for other maladies.

Hepatitis is easily spread through contact with the feces and urine of an infected dog. Your Beagle receives protection against this disease as part of the DHLPP series. However, most dogs recover after a brief illness without treatment.

Rabies

The rabies vaccine is the only one required by law because this very serious disease is easily transmitted to humans, often fatally, if not treated within the first two weeks of infection.

Rabies can be carried by a variety of wildlife, such as raccoons, foxes, skunks, and bats. Should one of these creatures bite a dog, the virus will more than likely be transmitted to him. However, with inoculation, the virus cannot infect the dog's central nervous system because the vaccine is 100 percent reliable.

Symptoms include extremely aggressive behavior, discharge from the eyes and nose, frothing around the mouth, staggering, and sensitivity to light and noise. Some dogs can become very weak and unresponsive. If not treated, an infected dog can die within days or weeks, as well as pose a risk to all who come in contact with him.

In many states, county officials keep track of dogs in their jurisdictions by issuing pet licenses only upon receiving notification of a rabies vaccination by an area veterinarian. This helps prevent or minimize rabies outbreaks, especially in rural areas.

Because it is the law, and because your Beagle will love running through the woods after interesting scents of small game, it is imperative that you get him inoculated as soon as possible.

NONCORE VACCINES

Noncore vaccines are considered optional, with the decision to administer them dependent on whether your dog might be exposed to certain diseases, some of which may be present only in your area, such as Lyme disease. Discuss the need for these with your veterinarian.

Bordetellosis

Bordetellosis, also known as kennel cough due to the commonality of infection while in close contact with other dogs, is caused by *bordetella* bacteria that attack the respiratory system. The bacteria can replicate within the lungs, sometimes resulting in pneumonia if not treated.

Symptoms include a hacking cough, sometimes accompanied by gagging or retching, with some frothing around the mouth. The symptoms can worsen with activity and excitement as lung function becomes impaired. Some dogs will also have a watery discharge from their eyes and nose.

Mild cases do not need to be treated with medication. However, antibiotics are indicated to prevent secondary infection due to overall impairment of the dog's natural antibodies.

If you plan on boarding your Beagle or taking him where there are other dogs who may be in close proximity to him, protect him with an annual *bordetella* vaccine.

Coronavirus

Coronavirus is highly contagious, especially to young and old dogs. It primarily infects the upper respiratory and gastrointestinal tract and manifests in similar ways to parvovirus but is not as dangerous. Symptoms include vomiting, diarrhea, and dehydration. While coronavirus is debilitating, it is not often fatal.

Treatment consists only of administration of IV fluids if the dog is dehydrated or medication to reduce diarrhea. Where coronavirus is a serious concern, you may want to discuss with your vet the option of having your young Beagle inoculated.

Leptospirosis

Leptospirosis is caused by many different strains of bacteria. These bacteria attack and damage a variety of body tissues, but they particularly like to grow in the kidneys and liver. Because infection is expelled in urine, it can reenter the environment and infect other dogs or wildlife that come into contact with it.

Symptoms of leptospirosis include lethargy, vomiting, diarrhea, and jaundice (yellowing of the skin). Without immediate antibiotic treatment, the dog will not be able to produce urine and will hemorrhage within his lungs and intestines.

As with rabies, lepto can infect humans. However, it is easily treated with antibiotics and will clear up within weeks with few latent repercussions.

Lyme Disease

Although not thoroughly tested and proven to be totally effective, the Lyme vaccine may prevent your dog from becoming infected with Lyme disease from a tick bite. Lyme disease can be difficult to diagnose without a blood test and, if not caught in time, can prove to be fatal. The only way you might be able to notice the beginning stages is that your dog is less active, does not want much attention, and seems to move as though his legs hurt. Some dogs become persnickety, suddenly becoming angry at a housemate with whom they might normally play on a regular basis. If symptoms show, or a blood test is positive, a prescription medication is used for one month, with most dogs showing improvement in several days.

BREED-SPECIFIC ILLNESSES

Beagles are a very healthy, hardy breed and, though popular, have not been line bred into frailty. However, as with most breeds, there are specific conditions common to Beagles of which you should be aware.

CHERRY EYE

Cherry eye is a swelling of the third eyelid. When this occurs, it protrudes due to infection and inflammation and becomes red. Antibiotics will normally treat the problem, but sometimes surgery is indicated if the problem repeats.

EPILEPSY

Epilepsy is a disorder that affects the brain and central nervous system. It is not common but does occur in Beagles. The symptoms are mainly seizures, disorientation, and behavior abnormalities. A Beagle who experiences a severe seizure will lose muscle control, stiffen, and convulse, which can be disconcerting to witness. Epilepsy usually worsens with age and must be controlled with prescription medication. As with most regular medications, dosages must gradually be increased as the dog's body builds a tolerance because the neural pathways change.

GLAUCOMA

Glaucoma is a disorder that causes pressure behind the eye, eventually damaging the optic nerve. The constant pressure will cause blindness if not treated with prescribed eye drops. Sometimes surgery is indicated as a means of restoring some lost eyesight.

This condition is generally genetic, and though breeders should avoid breeding dogs who have a history of glaucoma, they do not always recognize it in their breeding dogs.

HEART MURMUR

Some Beagles have an irregular heartbeat, also known as a heart murmur. This is caused by dilated cardiomyopathy or pulmonic stenosis. If your Beagle has a heart murmur, your veterinarian will recognize it during his annual examination. There really is not much you can do to treat this condition with medication, and it rarely

Intervertebral disk disease is common in Beagles, especially those with short legs and a long back. It causes neck or back pain, paralysis, and sometimes incontinence.

affects your Beagle overall, but control of your dog to ensure that he does not experience heart stress during activity is helpful.

INTERVERTEBRAL DISK DISEASE
Intervertebral disk disease is difficult to recognize until the dog begins yelping from pain when lifted or refuses to engage in strenuous activity such as climbing stairs. This malady affects the disks between your dog's vertebrae. As the condition advances, disks begin to collapse, putting pressure on the spinal cord. Your veterinarian will often prescribe anti-inflammatory medication to help with the pain, but it does not cure the problem. Extensive surgery may help but requires lots of rest afterward to allow for proper healing. Acupuncture can often help control the pain and inflammation as well.

PARASITES
There is hardly a means of avoiding parasitic infestation. Parasites are everywhere in the environment, and your Beagle loves to be outdoors in full exposure to numerous types of them. He can inadvertently walk over them, ingest them, rub against them, or receive a bite from them, and no topical defense can totally prevent exposure. You need to diligently check your dog regularly to ensure that any infestation does not achieve unhealthy levels. The only means of prevention is to use regular topical treatments, take fecal samples to your veterinarian every six months to check for internal parasites, and learn how to recognize physical signs of infestation.

EXTERNAL PARASITES
External parasites are far easier to detect than internal parasites, which cannot be detected until they affect the gastrointestinal system. External parasites leave clear signs of their presence.

Fleas
Fleas like warm, moist areas and will tend to congregate around your dog's back end, stomach, and neck. These are the areas that your Beagle will scratch, sometimes until the hair falls out.

You will be able to see fleas by carefully inspecting your Beagle's coat. You may also see flea dirt (little black specs), which is dried blood left behind by feeding fleas. Many dogs have allergies to flea saliva and will have raised, crusty skin around the bites.

Topical repellents are helpful but are not 100 percent effective. And what's really worrisome is that if you see one flea, there are thousands that you don't see! Eggs are laid on the animal, but they easily fall off into the environment onto carpeting, bedding, floorboards, and soil. And fleas reproduce rapidly—anywhere from two days to two weeks, depending on environmental conditions.

Not only do you need to use a flea comb each time your dog comes in from the outdoors, but you also need to dip the comb in alcohol to kill the fleas on the comb. If your dog is infested, remove him from the premises and take him to have a flea bath. You need to be vigilant about keeping your home environment free of fleas as well. Wash bedding and toys frequently; vacuum often, changing the vacuum bags frequently; and, if necessary, set off foggers in your home and car to kill adult fleas, which are not usually killed by insecticides. Use foggers again, if necessary, usually in ten days, to kill any fleas that may have hatched in the interim. To ensure that your dog does not bring in more hitchhikers from the outdoors, spray your yard with a pet-safe insecticide to kill eggs and larvae.

During warm months, there are more parasites and insects in the environment, making your Beagle more susceptible to infestation and bites. You must be proactive if you suspect infestation because getting rid of fleas is extremely difficult.

Mites

Mites are parasites that also are a cause of many skin problems (mange) on dogs. They burrow into the skin, lay eggs, and feed on your dog's blood, causing severe irritation with symptoms of inflammation, itching, and hair loss.

There are two types of mites: those that remain in the ears and those that infect the skin and produce demodectic mange and sarcoptic mange. Demodectic mange is normally inherited from the dog's mother, while sarcoptic mange is contracted through close contact with another infected animal. Symptoms of mange include patchy, dry, flaky skin and, sometimes, bare patches. Mange mites are difficult to get rid of. Eradication requires use of special medicated baths and topical creams.

Ear mites are crab-like parasites that live in the ear canals and sometimes on the head. They feed on skin debris and ear wax, causing inflammation that the body responds to by producing more wax. Ear mites are easily cured with ear medication.

Ticks

Ticks are very nasty parasites. They carry and transmit a number of bacterial diseases that can cause illness in your Beagle—and in you as well, if you're bitten by one that is infected. These illnesses include Lyme disease, Rocky Mountain spotted fever, tularemia, and encephalitis.

Ticks live in tall grasses and can easily latch onto your Beagle as he passes through. Not only do they attach themselves to your dog's skin and feed on his blood, but they will stay on the host until they've completed their meal, dispensing dangerous bacteria in the process. Coming in many varieties, they appear as small, flat, dark brown bugs. Most notably, the deer tick, which is barely larger than a grain of pepper, transmits Lyme disease, a flu-like illness that causes fatigue, fever, loss of appetite, and swollen neck glands.

Always check your dog for ticks and fleas after he has spent time outdoors.

Preventives and topical treatments will often kill these parasites once they land on and/or bite your dog. However, this will not prevent the transfer of any disease they may carry. It is not unheard of for protected dogs to have Lyme disease from tick bites. Only regular blood tests will help you know if your dog has been infected. And, between early spring and fall, check your dog from head to toe every day to discover any ticks that may have hitched a ride on him.

Careful removal of a tick is very important, as removal of only part of the parasite can still result in transmission of disease. Once removed, the tick must be dropped into alcohol to kill it.

Ringworm

Ringworm is a fungus that lives on your dog's skin. A dog with ringworm will have bare, scaly patches on his body that are very itchy. Unfortunately, this fungus can also infect people and is highly contagious to other animals who live in close contact with the infected animal.

Ringworm is easily treated with topical anti-fungal ointment and careful hygiene of all living areas.

INTERNAL PARASITES

Most dogs have worms at some point in their lives. Many get them from their mothers during gestation and nursing. Some dogs are infected through eating the waste deposits of other animals.

Roundworms and tapeworms are easily seen without a microscope, but others are not generally diagnosed until other physical reactions are apparent. These symptoms include diarrhea, blood in the stool, weight loss, dry fur, vomiting, and general poor appearance. However, there are some that cause few symptoms until they reach a large infestation level. Other internal parasite eggs remain dormant until times of stress, or as with roundworms, until latter stages of pregnancy.

Early diagnosis of internal parasites is essential for returning the dog to normal health without suffering permanent debilitating effects. The following are the most common.

Heartworms

The most insidious and dangerous internal parasites are heartworms. These parasites cause fatality if not discovered and treated. Heartworms are transmitted through mosquito bites. It can take months for symptoms to develop because the worms do not immediately invade the heart. Worm larvae first migrate through the blood to the heart, where they can grow to an impressive length within the heart vessels, eventually blocking them and shutting down the circulatory system.

Symptoms include coughing, weight loss, and lethargy; though by the time these symptoms manifest, it is likely that the dog's heart is engorged with heartworms.

Heartworm infestation is easily avoided with a monthly preventive given in tablet form. Before your veterinarian will prescribe the preventive, he will do a blood test to ensure that your Beagle is not already infected because giving this medication can complicate the situation making it worse. Should your dog be diagnosed with heartworms, the treatment is often painful and not always 100 percent effective. Prevention is the best course of action, and it is as easy as giving your dog a pill that tastes like a treat—and no Beagle turns down a tasty treat.

Hookworms

Hookworms attach themselves to the dog's intestine, where they ingest blood, causing their host to become anemic. As dogs often walk in unsanitary areas, there is a likelihood of contracting hookworms. The environment is not always the main culprit, however. Some pups are born with them, along with roundworms. This parasite is easily extricated through the use of deworming medicine. But that does not mean your dog cannot get them again. There are currently heartworm treatments that also offer monthly preventives for hookworms, whipworms, and roundworms. Prevention is the best medicine.

Roundworms

Roundworms are a common parasite. Most pups are born with them, whether or not their mother was dewormed. Because roundworms grow long and multiply quickly, they can cause sudden death if left untreated. Symptoms include a potbelly appearance, diarrhea, coughing, and vomiting. These worms are also transmittable to humans.

Pups should receive their first deworming at 5 weeks of age, to be followed up two weeks later in order to be fully cleared of the roundworms. Regular fecal testing will ensure that your Beagle does not harbor these parasites.

Tapeworms

Tapeworms are another type of parasite that is transmitted through flea saliva and the feces of other animals. They feed on the dog's intestine similarly to whipworms and hookworms. Although not as dangerous as the other internal parasites, they transmit just as easily. Because Beagles will often eat carrion that is infested with these parasites, it is a good idea to do regular fecal checks to ensure that your dog is not harboring them. Tapeworms look like little pieces of "rice" and appear in segments in his feces and around his anal region. They are easily eradicated with deworming medication.

Whipworms

Whipworms are very prevalent in the United States because they can survive upwards of five years in any environment, even without a host. They are transmitted through the feces of any infected host animal. For example, an infected rabbit can leave droppings in your dog's fenced yard. Should your dog snack on these droppings, he will contract these parasites.

Whipworms lodge themselves in the lower intestine. It can take many months for them to be detected. Symptoms include diarrhea, vomiting, anemia, and lethargy. Whipworms are easily treated with deworming medication and their development prevented through monthly treatments. Providing monthly treatment is important if your dog has experienced them at some point because they will remain in the environment for a long time, putting your Beagle constantly at risk of reinfestation.

Allergic reactions often manifest as excessive scratching, ear rubbing, bottom rubbing, sneezing, and dry, itchy skin.

COMMON AILMENTS

There are several maladies that your dog is likely to experience at some time during his life. Because Beagles love to follow their nose in pursuit of interesting scents, hunting up animals (both alive and dead!), their droppings, and other assorted debris, your Beagle will not only have to be regularly checked for worms, but sometimes what he eats will not agree with him. His digestive system will become irritated, causing diarrhea or other problems. Your Beagle may also experience allergic reactions to foods or to environmental factors. Or he may be afflicted by other health issues that plague all dogs.

Regardless of what you believe may have caused your dog's ailments, always take him to the veterinarian to ensure that he receives appropriate treatment—especially if whatever is occurring does not clear up within a few days.

The following are just a few of the more common issues that may affect your dog.

ALLERGIES

Allergic reactions often manifest as excessive scratching, ear rubbing, bottom rubbing, sneezing, and dry coat. These reactions can occur from insect bites, parasite infestations, and any number of environmental factors. However, some of the most common and controllable allergens are in commercial diets. Often, dogs are allergic to corn, wheat, soy, oatmeal, or rice. The only way to know for certain if your Beagle is allergic to any of these foods is to have your veterinarian do an allergy test. The results will guide you in how to feed your dog so that you can minimize some of his adverse reactions.

DIARRHEA

Dogs can get diarrhea for a variety of reasons. It may be caused by certain illnesses, internal parasites, bacteria invading the gastrointestinal tract, or allergies to food or medicine. A foreign mass in the intestine—whether biological or something swallowed by your dog—can also cause diarrhea. Something as seemingly benign as suddenly changing the diet can also be the culprit.

The most likely cause of sudden diarrhea in Beagles is likely due to eating something that does not agree with them. If this occurs just after a walk in the woods, the cause may be due to having eaten rabbit or deer feces, fungus, or a poisonous plant. Another likely cause could be stress. Some timid Beagles are easily stressed, which causes gastrointestinal malfunction.

The best course of action is to take a fecal sample to your veterinarian for testing as soon as possible because continued diarrhea can cause dehydration and rapid weight loss. This way you can discover the source of the problem immediately and offer appropriate treatment. Sometimes, however, bacteria does not survive outside the dog's body during testing, which is common for giardia infections, and a specific course of action may not be focused on the true cause and therefore may not be successful. Testing for giardia infections usually requires that a fecal sample be taken directly from the anus and immediately tested for best results. Your vet will determine the best course of action based on information you can provide, symptoms, and test results.

Knowing how to recognize potential health problems and how to handle them is vital to your dog's overall well-being.

If diarrhea is mild, offer only meat broth for 12 to 24 hours. The next day, you can begin feeding your Beagle a bland diet of cooked rice and chicken for a few days. Often, a veterinarian will prescribe this diet regardless of the reason for the diarrhea because it will help the digestive system heal and return to normal more quickly. It is always best to consult with your vet regarding the best course of action to take because ongoing diarrhea can have serious consequences and may even result in death.

EAR INFECTIONS

Ear infections are common in dogs with heavy, folded-over ear flaps. Although Beagles do not experience these infections as much as many retrievers, they can still occur. Cleaning your dog's ears weekly will help prevent this. A good herbal cleanser will both clean and disinfect the outer ear. Sometimes, however, detritus gets into the ear canal, causing a more serious problem that requires professional help. Particles can hold in bacteria that might otherwise dissipate, causing an infection. Symptoms include redness, itching, and a foul odor. Once your veterinarian determines the type of infectious material, he will prescribe an ear ointment for daily application. It normally takes from seven to ten days to totally clear up an ear infection. Because they are often painful and can cause permanent damage to the inner ear if left untreated, ear infections are best prevented from occurring by practicing good hygiene.

INSECT BITES AND STINGS

During the warmer months, we are all subject to the wrath of stinging and biting insects. With all that your Beagle will be pushing at with his nose, he is likely to get stung. Unless he is having an allergic reaction, you can utilize the same procedures you would for yourself or a child: Clean the sting site well, and apply a baking soda paste. Afterward, some antibiotic cream should be applied to prevent infection. Sometimes, buffered aspirin is helpful in managing pain and inflammation, but you must always check with your vet before giving it to your dog, as it can be toxic.

SPAYING/NEUTERING

If you are not a professional Beagle breeder, you should have your dog neutered or spayed. It's that simple. With the huge surplus of unwanted pets in this world, there is no reason that you should add to the overpopulation problem by allowing your beloved Beagle to go through the stress and the associated health risks of having puppies. Male Beagles, in particular, are in danger if left intact because they will go to extremes to escape, digging under fencing and traveling a long distance to reach a female dog in estrus. Your male dog is not only at risk from competing male dogs but also from vehicles as he crosses roads and has encounters with wild animals in the woods, poisons in neighboring yards, and unfriendly strangers that may not appreciate his presence on their property or around their pets. Your dog might be caught and taken to an animal shelter where he will be exposed to other dogs who might harbor disease and parasites, as well as being exposed to the high stress level of upset animals.

A neutered/spayed dog makes a better pet, one who is less likely to want to wander seeking other dogs, though you should provide play dates with other canines on a regular basis. A Beagle who has been neutered/spayed will be more likely to remain at home and be relaxed. He will also be less likely to mark inside the house or even throughout his yard. Moreover, neutered/spayed Beagles will have fewer internal problems as they age because the reproductive system of dogs left intact can be vulnerable to age-related infections and abnormalities.

ALTERNATIVE THERAPIES

While modern medical treatments began just a mere 300 years ago, the holistic approach to illness, injury, and infection has been used to treat human ailments for more than 7,000 years. These ancient therapies, which are now referred to as alternative or holistic therapies, include acupuncture, chiropractic, herbs, flower essences, and aromatherapy. All these approaches work within the body to develop antibodies and release chemicals to help it heal itself. From targeting specific nerves to deaden pain and promote healing to manipulating body parts, alternative approaches can often better target the root cause of a problem instead of merely treating the manifested symptoms.

Alternative therapies are becoming more popular for use with pets and can be an option before resorting to more invasive treatments. Often, a combination of conventional medicine and alternative therapies can be adopted.

ACUPUNCTURE

Acupuncture is based on the principle that life energy, which flows from the body's organs, can be disturbed by injury or illness. Using fine needles to stimulate these energy paths, called meridians, the energy stream can be restored, ultimately curing the malady.

This form of ancient Chinese medicine is used to treat a variety of disorders of the musculoskeletal, reproductive, and neurological systems. It is also used to treat skin diseases.

Dog Tale

Alternative therapies work well for behavioral abnormalities. For example, a specific combination of flower essences can be used to take the edge off of separation anxiety or reactivity. Massage also is commonly used as a calmative for distressed dogs. Through combined therapies, the dog can relax and heal faster, both mentally and physically.

I have often boarded Beagles who have separation anxiety. Some display excessive panting and whining; others are overly pushy or assertive. After consulting with the dog's guardians, I use a combination of flower essences, along with aromatherapy to aid in calming the dog. I always keep a lavender diffuser in the main part of my kennel building, along with hormone diffusers in the suites of dogs who have anxiety issues. Though this merely takes the edge off, with the help of calming massage and lots of exercise, the dog soon calms down, settles in, and enjoys his kennel stay.

I find it helpful to use patience and noninvasive methods rather than forceful measures to help a dog through a difficult experience.

Veterinary acupuncturists believe that these treatments strengthen a dog's immune system, relieve pain, and improve body function. Acupuncture is often used when a dog has problems such as arthritis, chronic pain and inflammation of any sort, paralysis, and gastrointestinal disorders. It has been proven to relieve muscle spasms and release endorphins (the "feel good" hormone), and therefore it is sometimes used to improve athletic performance.

CHIROPRACTIC/MASSAGE

Chiropractic and massage therapies involve using touch and manipulation to diagnose, treat, and prevent disease.

Essentially, chiropractic therapy consists of spinal manipulations to correct subluxations, or places where the spine is out of alignment. A misalignment of the spine can cause organ, muscle, and nerve malfunction, as well as break down bone structure. Because Beagles are athletic dogs, they can easily be injured when running, jumping, or climbing. Something as simple as racing down stairs, or being locked in a small crate for too long during travel, can cause a subluxation. Active performance Beagles may step the wrong way on an agility course or just play rough with other dogs and become injured. Chiropractic offers a stress-relieving alternative to expensive, invasive surgery. Often the spine can be realigned through a series of sessions and reduced activity for a short time. When the spine and other parts of the skeletal system function smoothly, the entire system of bones, joints, and muscles works in harmony.

Massage has many therapeutic uses. It stimulates circulation, disperses pain, and helps restore mobility and flexibility. It lowers stress hormones, increases the amount of oxygen that reaches tissues, and flushes out toxins and waste. Different forms of massage are used, depending on the dog's particular needs. Besides physical healing, massage also has proven helpful when a dog is stressed, frightened, or anxious.

HERBAL REMEDIES

Herbal remedies are derived by isolating the medicinal parts of plants and natural ingredients to treat and heal specific conditions and to support wellness. They can be prepared for either internal or external use, but most often, remedies taken internally are safest for dogs. Herbal remedies also are used for behavior modification. Many of these remedies have their roots in ancient medicine but have been advanced scientifically in their current form.

Practitioners who advocate herbal remedies do so not only because they are derived from natural substances, but because they are less invasive than modern pharmaceuticals. Another advantage is that whereas traditional veterinary medicine targets relief of symptoms, herbal remedies target the source of the illness, thereby exterminating the symptoms without medications that often have debilitating side effects. For example, when treating arthritis, a typical course of action is to prescribe a remedy with natural anti-inflammatory properties such as a sea mussel tincture, which provides nutrition and supports cartilage production, thereby relieving joint pain. Or instead of prescribing antibiotics for kennel cough, the herbal/homeopathic approach would be to give bromium, drosera, and aconite, which would aid in boosting the immune system and lessening mucous production. For a behavioral problem such as anxiety, the use of valerian, passion flower, and skullcap, as well as aromatherapy with lavender, aid in calming the dog.

Herbal remedies work best when given to a dog directly in the mouth on an empty stomach, such as before mealtime. This allows the ingredients to be thoroughly absorbed by the blood and distributed throughout the dog's system quickly.

This type of treatment requires more time and effort than just giving a pill or inoculation. Herbal remedies need to be administered often, over the course of several days to weeks, depending on the condition being treated. Though herbal

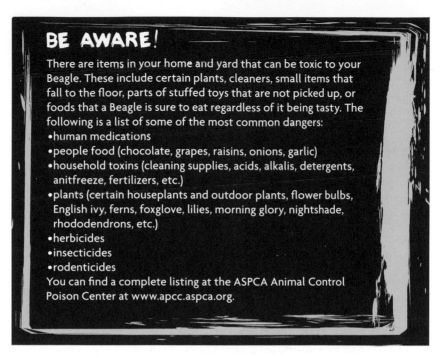

BE AWARE!

There are items in your home and yard that can be toxic to your Beagle. These include certain plants, cleaners, small items that fall to the floor, parts of stuffed toys that are not picked up, or foods that a Beagle is sure to eat regardless of it being tasty. The following is a list of some of the most common dangers:
- human medications
- people food (chocolate, grapes, raisins, onions, garlic)
- household toxins (cleaning supplies, acids, alkalis, detergents, anitfreeze, fertilizers, etc.)
- plants (certain houseplants and outdoor plants, flower bulbs, English ivy, ferns, foxglove, lilies, morning glory, nightshade, rhododendrons, etc.)
- herbicides
- insecticides
- rodenticides

You can find a complete listing at the ASPCA Animal Control Poison Center at www.apcc.aspca.org.

supplements can be found at your local pet store, consult a holistic veterinarian who understands the tenets behind herbal medicine and recognizes a dog's sensitivities to certain herbs before giving them to your Beagle.

FIRST AID

Just as you have a first-aid kit for you and your family, so should you prepare one for your Beagle. This will ensure that you are ready for emergencies—and you can be sure your curious little dog will put his nose in the wrong place from time to time. Beagles are naturally inquisitive and outgoing, facing new events with their typical boldness.

Here is a list of all the items you should have in your kit:

- adhesive tape or self-sticking vet wrap
- aloe vera gel (to soothe burns and other irritations)
- antibacterial ointment
- canine antidiarrheal medication
- canine first-aid manual
- cotton balls and cotton swabs (for cleaning and application of medication)

- hydrogen peroxide (for cleaning wounds)
- instant hot/cold packs
- nonstick gauze pads, gauze
- rectal thermometer
- saline solution
- styptic powder
- tweezers and scissors

If you travel with your dog, especially on outdoor hiking or camping trips, bring along a basic first-aid kit. Always have some fresh water, antiseptic wipes, sterile gauze pads, vet wrap, antibacterial ointment, and tweezers.

In the event that your Beagle shows signs of injury, whether at home or away from home, try to apply first aid, keep him as comfortable as possible, and rush him to your veterinarian. If he's bleeding, clean the area with hydrogen peroxide and apply pressure to stop the bleeding. Wrapping your dog in a blanket will help him feel more secure, prevent him from moving and causing further injury to himself, and keep him from losing body heat, which can result from serious injury (especially when the dog is in shock).

HEALTH CARE FOR SENIORS

Older dogs have their own specific health problems of which you should be aware. Seniors face common issues related to aging, such as arthritis pain, gastrointestinal distress, loss of hearing and/or eyesight, and sometimes partial loss of sense of smell. Some may also face more serious problems, such as cancer, dementia, and depression.

It can be difficult to discern early signs of these changes because dogs strive to cover up their weaknesses. You may not notice your Beagle going blind until you see the cataracts forming on his eyes, turning them cloudy. You may not recognize when your dog is starting to favor a leg or has trouble with his back until he refuses to traverse

Your dog's overall quality of life should be the most important factor you consider as he advances in age.

steps or no longer hops about when you come home. Hearing loss can be even more difficult to discern because you may believe your Beagle is merely being selective about his responses, such as not coming when called, which has happened regularly throughout his lifetime anyway.

Regardless of your Beagle showing arthritis pain or becoming ornery when played with, continuing to exercise him regularly helps his muscles support his bone structure, giving him a longer, more mobile life. However, instead of taking him on long walks, try several shorter ones. Your Beagle will still enjoy his time with you. You can also give him joint supplements that will help lubricate his joints, and as he worsens, the veterinarian can prescribe anti-inflammatory medication.

Some dogs will get cancer in their senior years. Through yearly blood scans, you may be able to detect the early signs before it becomes fatal. When your Beagle reaches his senior years, around the age of 7 or 8, request that he be tested so that your veterinarian has a baseline and can keep track of any changes in his chemical levels and organ efficacy. Changes can denote the presence of cancer or other diseases.

As Beagles age, they tend to become more sensitive and irritable at times. This is due to discomfort from arthritis or other similar issues and sometimes the decline of their senses, such as hearing or eye sight. This also can result from canine cognitive dysfunction (CCD), or dementia. Your dog may pace, appear distracted, or not sleep normally. Some dogs become incontinent or merely forget why they went to their relief area, returning inside to do their business. When CCD becomes advanced, your dog may not wish to spend time with you anymore and is often disoriented. Some dogs may even become aggressive, especially if suddenly awakened. Your patience will help, as will guiding your dog a little more closely. Sometimes giving him extra exercise just before bedtime will help him sleep better.

If your dog has recently lost a playmate, he can become depressed. This will manifest in a variety of behaviors, including excessive barking, anxiety, destructiveness, aggression, or being very clingy. Depression can also occur with CCD.

There are medications available to help your older Beagle cope. Discuss this with your veterinarian at length. You may need to try one or two before you see a discernable improvement.

Senior Beagles go through many physical and emotional changes. To keep your older dog healthy and happy, you may need to make changes to his diet, exercise routines, and overall care. Having him examined by his veterinarian twice each year instead of once is another good wellness measure.

TRAINING YOUR
BEAGLE

All living creatures communicate information in one form or another. Humans have developed hundreds of languages and dialects, both in spoken and written form. Animals also communicate with each other in various ways. In order to properly train an animal, we must use a form of communication they understand. Dogs are one of the easiest animals for humans to communicate with because they are receptive to vocalizations and body language, which we can interpret because we use these forms of communicating as well. We are also at an advantage because canine communication has been studied for a long time and, more often than not, is well understood by animal professionals.

We've learned that dogs communicate using all their senses. They use vocal tones, visual cues, posturing, and scenting. Varying combinations of these elements have specific meanings to other dogs. To most of us humans, however, much of what dogs indicate when they move their bodies or vocalize in a certain way is mumbo jumbo. And vice versa. Therefore, in order for us to train a dog, we need to first understand what he is conveying with his instinctual communication techniques, which are actually quite basic and fixed. There are no gray areas in canine "language," nor do meanings vary depending on the context of the circumstances. To dogs, things are either accepted or not accepted by the pack. Dogs don't hold grudges or try to get even. They don't understand inconsistencies. They prefer structure, routine, and rules they can live by. Dogs need to know what is expected of them at all times. Without these boundaries, they develop anxieties, and sometimes this turns into a desire to take over the pack and run things themselves. They need leadership. Training not only bridges the communication gap between dogs and humans, but it also strengthens bonds and sets the rules.

Most dogs are far happier as followers—pack members—than as leaders. A follower can relax, knowing that the leader will take

Basic obedience commands create a simple language between pet owners and their dogs.

care of things. A canine leader will always be on edge over territorial disputes, food procurement, and maintaining order within the rest of the pack. Which job seems easier to you: following your Beagle wherever he may lead, which may involve some long-term quests through the woods, or teaching your Beagle to follow you along the trail and remain with you so that you enjoy your walks together? Training benefits both dogs and their human family members.

POSITIVE TRAINING TECHNIQUES

The best training method to use with your Beagle—or any dog—is positive reinforcement. This means that he will be rewarded whenever he offers appropriate behavior. Pairing a cue (command) and an appropriate response will ensure that your dog *wants* to do the right thing instead of being forced to do so. A Beagle trained with these methods will be far more cooperative than one who is trained by force or who is verbally or physically punished into behaving, such as being dragged around via a neck collar or yelled at.

One method of positive training, called operant conditioning, has been used for over a century in training many species, as well as in teaching humans. It's a means of presenting a stimulus (a cue such as a hand signal or verbal command) and teaching a specific pattern of responses in order to earn a reward. As the pattern is learned, it gradually increases in complexity, teaching the student in a positive manner at his own rate of learning.

Modern operant conditioning is reward based, not correction based. This is not to say that your Beagle will never need a correction at any time. That's not realistic. There are many behaviors that are self-rewarding, and your dog will need to be redirected away from unwanted behaviors by replacing them instead with appropriate behaviors. A good example of this is jumping up. Beagles can be very persistent in this behavior because the mere act itself is enjoyable to them. In the case of the jumping bean Beagle, it's necessary to understand that this is an attention-seeking behavior. Therefore, if you withdraw attention, your Beagle will no longer find that jumping up delivers the response he wants and will stop. After he stops jumping, redirect him into a sit and reward him for doing so by giving him attention, thus setting a good pattern to replace the bad one. This is a means of positive redirection rather than punishment.

No matter what you are trying to teach your dog, you can break it down into small components and shape the total behavior in such a way that your dog can learn and be encouraged by his success. Some dogs will learn in large steps; others will need training broken down into small steps. Because Beagles are eager learners, you'll most probably find that your dog will learn faster than you expect.

Socializing your dog to a variety of new people, pets, and places ensures that he will become a confident and well-adjusted adult.

SOCIALIZATION

Socialization is a means of acclimating your dog to his environment. Whether he lives in a suburban, urban, or rural neighborhood, he must learn to accept everyone and everything inhabiting it. Until he has been properly socialized, a dog will not be comfortable dealing with new and unfamiliar people and places and will not have a solid foundation for learning.

HOW TO SOCIALIZE YOUR DOG

The best means of acclimating your Beagle to all types of experiences is to expose him to them gradually. However, you need to make each encounter with something new positive for him, especially when he is going through the formative period between 4 and 18 months.

On your pup's first few outings away from home, make sure he is not stepped on while walking along the sidewalk. Redirect him away from anything that might be dangerous to his health. Allow him to greet others without fuss. Maintain a loose leash when he moves to greet other dogs, provided the meeting is agreed upon by the other dog's human companions. If not, redirect him by turning in the opposite direction and coaxing him to your side using a toy, food lure, or an enthusiastic tone of voice. Never get upset with him because he will sense your mood and become anxious. Always remain upbeat and happy. This will aid in his relaxation when confronted with new experiences.

If something frightens your little guy, bring lots of treats with you the next time you are certain to confront that object. As you gradually near the object, offer your pup treats and praise to keep his mind on you and away from the object he fears. When you are near enough, place a treat on the object and allow your pup to sniff it at his own pace and retrieve his reward as you praise and encourage him. Repeat this as often as needed for him to no longer fear the object. Take this approach with new people or other animals should he appear fearful of them.

If living in an urban environment, your Beagle will need to be comfortable with dense traffic, city sounds, passersby, other dogs, people carrying things, smells of food wafting through the doors of eateries, refuse left on the ground, and much more.

In a suburban environment, your pup might encounter a bit of vehicular traffic but mostly children and other people. Most Beagles love people of all ages, so there should not be any issue. However, there are some rescued Beagles who might be fearful of new people. As with acclimation to new, feared objects, give the new person some treats to offer your dog. Within a short time, your Beagle will think of this person as a treat dispenser instead of someone to be feared. Beagles quickly warm up to those who give them food.

In a rural environment, you will encounter a totally different type of situation—farm animals, farm equipment, and wildlife. While there is not much you can do to control the wildlife, you can teach your dog to respect cows, horses, and other farm animals, as well as not fear the sound of machinery. As with approaching novel objects in the city, you should use the same positive reinforcement methods. The main difference will be that farm animals make noises much unlike a stationary garbage can or elevator. If farm animal sounds are a source of insecurity, try offering treats while the cows are lowing for their breakfast or when the horses whinny for dinner. Always create a way of making each experience positive and then allowing your dog to take his time to investigate the source and discover how benign, or even enjoyable, it might be.

CRATE TRAINING

Training your Beagle to accept and enjoy his crate is very important. Not only will the crate keep him safe from harm and your home safe from him, but it will also keep your little sniffer in your good graces.

As crates simulate a dogs den, your Beagle will be willing to go inside and, if there's a comfy bed, use the crate for his napping spot. For a dog who is unwilling to enter the crate, throwing in treats and allowing him access to enter and exit at will makes the crate more inviting and conditions him to accept it as a safe haven.

HOW TO CRATE TRAIN

To help your Beagle get used to his crate, shape the behavior slowly and at his pace. Never shove him inside and close the door or you will further feed into his fear. Forcing the issue never works well. Beagles are fairly sensitive and have good memories.

To begin, sit on the floor with your dog and throw a treat inside the crate. Praise him as he enters, and greet him enthusiastically when he returns to you. Continue this until you see that he decides to remain inside waiting for you to throw in another treat. Of course, do so and praise your dog some more as that is exactly the behavior you sought.

To train your puppy to accept and enjoy his crate, introduce it gradually.

Next, throw in a treat or two and close the door briefly. Continually praise your dog enthusiastically, and put another treat inside the crate. Open the door and allow your Beagle to make the choice of either exiting the crate or remaining inside. If he chooses to remain inside, throw in another treat. If he comes out, no problem; move on to a different activity. Resume training a little later. Throw a treat into the crate, and allow him to enter to retrieve it and briefly close the door just as before.

At first, leave the crate door closed for a mere 20 seconds. Then gradually add an additional 10 seconds as your dog accepts the situation. Once you reach 3 minutes, you can begin extending the time your dog remains behind closed doors to 5 minutes, then 10, 15, and 20. During this time, remain nearby, and if your dog is quiet and plays with a toy, offer a couple of treats every now and then. If he's noisy, ignore him until he is quiet, then reward him and allow him to exit the crate. Never reward your Beagle for excessive barking or whining. Beagles tend to be vociferous anyway, and rewarding this behavior will increase this tendency.

When your dog is able to remain calmly and quietly in his crate with you nearby, begin to leave the room briefly, then return and reward him. Gradually build on this with each success, teaching your dog to remain calm inside his crate.

HOUSETRAINING

Once you have acclimated your Beagle to his crate, the housetraining process will be much easier. Meanwhile, the best way to begin is with routine, schedule, and consistency. Dogs are creatures of habit. The sooner they learn the routine and how to earn rewards, the sooner they will be far more relaxed and happy.

Take into consideration your personal schedule. When do you get up, eat your meals, go to work or school, and return home? Your Beagle needs to learn these routines, and you need to attend to your dog's needs consistently so that he will learn when and where to relieve himself.

Here is a sample schedule that you can easily change to suit your needs:

• 6:00 am: Take your dog to his relief area. [Note: Puppies need to be taken to their relief area every hour to hour and a half.]
• 6:30 am: Feed your dog.
• 7:00 am: Take your dog to his relief area.
• 10:00 am: Take your dog to his relief area.
• 12:00 pm: Puppies under 4 months old must be fed at midday.
• 2:00 pm: Take your dog to his relief area.
• 5:00 pm: Take your dog to his relief area.
• 5:30 pm: Feed your dog.
• 6:00 pm: Take your dog to his relief area.
• 9:00 pm: Take your dog to his relief area.

While puppies should be taken to their relief area frequently in order to avoid house soiling, a dog over the age of 6 months can be well attended by going six times each day. Puppies have a faster metabolism, hence must potty more often. As their metabolism slows and their meals reduce from three times per day to twice each day, they will not need to relieve themselves as often.

HOW TO HOUSETRAIN: POTTY ON COMMAND

Wouldn't it be nice to have your Beagle potty when you use a specific cue? That's certainly much better than waiting and waiting as he sniffs and meanders and plays instead of getting down to business. Teaching your dog to potty on cue will greatly enhance your communication process and save loads of time.

Begin by taking some food treats with you when you go to your dog's relief

BE AWARE!

While female dogs often complete their potty outing quickly, males tend to take longer, especially if they are not neutered because they like to scent mark along the way. Also, young male Beagles may have a tendency not to finish completely before you are ready to bring them back into the house because they can become distracted by a scent. Make certain to learn exactly how many times your dog will urinate so that you can prevent accidents indoors. It is typical for young male Beagles to urinate three or more times at any relief outing.

Also keep in mind that while you are housetraining your dog, he is sure to pick up on the fact that he will earn treats when he potties. He may try to potty at an inappropriate time and place, testing to see if this earns rewards as well. Beagles are always driven by food and will do anything to earn it. They may also try to go more often in order to earn even more rewards. Make certain that your dog doesn't finish too quickly, before he is really done, because you use praise and offer the reward too soon. You will learn to recognize when your Beagle has completely emptied his bladder and bowels. Be sure not to reinforce inappropriate behavior and to reward your dog only when you are sure he is finished.

area first thing in the morning. Your Beagle must have to go after having spent the night in his crate or was otherwise contained while you slept. The moment you reach his potty area, use a verbal cue, such as "potty," "business," or "do it," in an exuberant tone of voice.

Your dog is bound to go at some point. When he does so, praise him in a happy tone of voice and give him a treat when he finishes. Always use the same word when you reach his potty area, and always praise and give him treats at the precise moment that he is done. You can be sure that your Beagle will easily identify his actions with earning rewards.

Ring a Bell

Wouldn't it be great if your Beagle could tell you when he needs to potty? Teaching him how to ring a bell is exactly that. As most pet owners miss the subtler signs of the "potty dance," such as circling, sniffing, standing at the door and barking, or staring and whining, this is just the ticket to communicating the message loud and clear.

Hang a bell from the doorknob of the door you always walk through when taking your Beagle to his relief area. Before going through the door, allow your dog to lick off a bit of cheese or peanut butter that you rubbed onto the bell. The moment the bell makes noise, go through the door to your dog's relief area. Use the potty cue, praise, and reward him in a timely fashion to reinforce his good behavior.

Within a week or less, your Beagle will be ringing this bell. Beware, though, of his ringing it to garner attention instead of just letting you know that he needs to potty. Some dogs learn to do this when being ignored and wanting to play, and they've learned that you jump to your feet and take them for a walk when they touch the bell. To reduce the incidence of this, make sure you heed your dog's bell ringing only when you know that it is his potty time. This may mean temporarily removing the bell from the door between those times.

BASIC COMMANDS

Every dog should know basic commands. The main commands are *sit, come, down, stay,* and *heel.* Without this training, your Beagle will be difficult to live

Consistent positive training is necessary if you want to have a friendly, well-behaved dog.

with. Beagles can be strong-willed and especially indifferent to your cues when scenting. Teaching your dog early and consistently will ensure that he will listen to you instead of wandering off and finding trouble.

TARGETING

All training should begin with targeting. This is a means of teaching your dog to pay attention to you immediately through the use of positive reinforcement.

Begin by placing a treat, such as freeze-dried liver, chicken jerky, or another smelly piece of wholesome food, in your hand. Close your hand around the food and present your closed hand in front of your dog's face. He will have an instant attraction to your hand and try to get at the food. The moment he touches your hand with his nose (not his teeth!), mark that behavior with a special sound, such as saying "Yes" enthusiastically. Open your hand and give your dog the reward.

Repeat this several times, until your Beagle immediately recognizes what your closed hand means. Then, move your hand up and down. If your dog follows the motion with his head, mark the moment with your special sound or word, and reward him. Next, try side to side. Again mark the moment when he has moved his head a couple times.

The first step in training is to teach your dog to reliably pay attention to you on command.

Gradually build on this targeting behavior by moving your hand in different directions. Request more and more of a response by adding to the criteria prior to marking the moment and rewarding. For example, begin with a short head motion. Next move your hand in a wider arc. When your dog follows this well, move your hand even farther so that he must actually follow your hand with his entire body in order to attempt to put his nose on it. When he does this reliably, he is ready to learn basic obedience commands.

THE *SIT* COMMAND

The *sit* command will reinforce the first understanding of attentiveness. It will also briefly halt your Beagle from his current activity. Once redirected away from a behavior you don't want, you can direct him into a behavior you do want. For example, if he is racing after a child who just rode by on a bike, you can redirect his attention to

you in an orderly and positive manner by telling him to sit.

You can also use the *sit* as a default behavior. This means that your dog must do something for you, such as sit prior to receiving attention or his meals. This is far better than having your Beagle jumping on you and otherwise being annoying in order to attain these things. Control through the sit behavior is far more positive than frustration and annoyance.

How to Teach the *Sit*

The *sit* command is easily taught through targeting. All you'll need is time and some treats.

1. Place your target hand directly between your Beagle's eyes just out of reach over his head.
2. As his nose rises up, his rear end will lower.
3. The moment he sits, mark the behavior by opening your hand to give him his reward.
4. After two to three repetitions, you can begin saying "Sit" as you do this targeting exercise. Your Beagle will soon learn two cues: the visual cue of your hand over his head and the verbal cue, "Sit."

If you request the *sit* prior to any event, such as going through a door, receiving attention, putting on the leash, and before receiving a meal, you will gain a huge step in bridging the communication gap between you and your Beagle. Always keep training sessions short—five or ten minutes several times throughout the day—positive, and fun.

THE *COME* COMMAND

Teaching your dog to come to you when called is one of the most important commands and one of the most difficult for any Beagle hot on a trail to accomplish. Most Beagles would prefer to continue following a scent, and turning away from this instinctual behavior is less rewarding. Yet, the *come* is of ultimate importance because the ability to come can remove him from a dangerous situation, such as encountering a less agreeable animal or stepping in front of a moving car. Most important, associating the *come* command strictly with positive situations is the only means of helping your dog make the correct choice between coming to you and continuing on his merry way.

How to Teach the *Come*

To teach this command, you'll need some treats and a few of your Beagle's favorite toys.

1. Begin by placing your target hand, with a treat inside, in front of your dog's nose.
2. The moment he moves to touch your hand, step backward and lower your upper body at the same time. This is an attractive gesture to a dog, giving him incentive to follow you.
3. When you see him moving toward you, stop, allow him to touch your hand, and give him his reward.
4. Repeat this exercise, gradually increasing your steps backward so that your Beagle must move more to reach you.
5. Once your visual cue is clear, begin adding the verbal cue (command), such as the word "come" or "here," using a happy, enthusiastic tone. This helps to praise your Beagle as he's moving toward you and further encourages him to respond correctly.
6. As your dog learns the verbal command, begin increasing the criteria for his rewards by making him come to you from farther and farther away.
7. When your dog is reliably working this command without any distractions, gradually add some. For example, place a few of his toys in the area where you are training him. When he gets to the point of ignoring his toys, try having a person or two in the area. Working outside is also a great distraction because there are numerous attractive sights and smells everywhere.

THE *DOWN* COMMAND

Once your Beagle has learned how to come and sit, it is time to teach him how to lie down on command. This is an important behavior—as well as a means of earning tummy rubs!—because he needs to learn how to settle down and relax. Speaking of tummy rubs, this is a sure method of getting an instant down. Merely rub your dog's tummy, and he'll likely lie down so that you can implement your training. Be sure to praise this action and pair it with a verbal cue such as "Down" so that he will learn the cue faster. However, if you wish to use a more formal training method, instead of relying on a chance occurrence, use your targeting techniques.

How to Teach the *Down*

To teach this command, all you'll need are some treats.
1. Place your hand, with a treat in it, under your Beagle's nose.
2. As you lower your hand, his nose will follow. Some Beagles will automatically

Dog Tale

When I begin training a Beagle to come when called, I like to use a game format called Round Robin. I place all the dog guardians approximately 10 feet (3 m) apart in a circle. They all take turns calling their dog to come to them. To add variation, I instruct them to cue the dog to perform other behaviors, such as *stay* or *down*. This adds to the fun and teaches the Beagle to do more than respond to a pattern. Using a game also is a great means of teaching children to communicate with their dog effectively. The dog has so much fun that he often anticipates who will call him next. This positive experience transfers to other situations as well, with the dog eagerly responding to the *come* command from all family members even when otherwise engaged—such as when he is busy scenting.

go down; some won't. For the dog who does follow your hand all the way down, instantly reward.

3. Begin adding the "Down" verbal cue after several repetitions.
4. For a Beagle who does not go down all the way, gradually increase the criteria with each success. For example, begin with rewarding head lowering. When he does so readily, praise and reward him only when he begins to lower his upper body. As he starts to respond automatically by lowering his upper body, hold out on praising him until he begins to lower his rear end. Sometimes inching the treat a little forward (not by much, though) will help him reach for his target and thereby lower his entire body.

Your Beagle will quickly learn how to earn his rewards, so the *down* command will not be difficult once he has a full understanding of your visual and verbal cues.

THE *STAY* COMMAND

The *stay* command will likely be the most difficult behavior for your Beagle to learn. This is not a sedate breed. Beagles love to move about and find fun activities. However, it is important to teach your dog to perform *stays* in situations that may be dangerous to him or those in which he may become overexcited and inadvertently injure someone, such as at open doors, prior to crossing the street, when allowing children to interact with him, or when being groomed.

How to Teach the *Stay*

To teach this command, you'll need some treats, a harness, and a leash. Be sure to make the *stay* exercises easy and fun for your dog.

1. Begin by putting your dog into a *sit* or *down* and waiting just a moment or two prior to giving him his reward.

2. Gradually increase the time between asking for the *sit* and offering the reward as your Beagle remains in place successfully. If he gets a little antsy, reduce the amount of time you wait before offering the reward. You don't want your dog to stop performing the correct behavior, so reducing the time you ask him to remain in place allows him to be successful. For example, if you are trying to wait six seconds prior to giving him the reward, but he moves a bit after the fifth second, go back to five seconds or less if needed, and repeat this exercise until your Beagle is reliable. Then gradually add another second or two.

3. When your Beagle can reliably remain in place for at least ten seconds prior to getting his reward, it is time to add the *stay* cue. Use both a hand and verbal cue, so that later, you can use one or the other, depending on the situation. A good hand cue for the *stay* is showing your dog an open palm. There's no need to touch his face or to bring your hand toward him. Merely show him your open palm, then take the visual cue away. Then use the word "stay" or "wait" as a verbal cue.

4. To improve your dog's response, praise him as he remains in place. Verbal praise acts as a "keep doing a good job" communiqué, encouraging your Beagle to continue, knowing that his reward is on the way.

5. When your Beagle can perform a *stay* for upwards of 30 seconds with you remaining stationary, begin to add some slight movement around him. A shuffle from side to side is a good way to begin, with additional movement, staying close, as he accepts it. Again, if he starts to break his *stay*, go back a few steps to a point at which he was performing well, and repeat the exercise until he is reliable before adding any more distance.

6. Once your Beagle can stay in both the *sit* and *down* positions with you moving around him, you can begin adding more distance. Do this very gradually, and be sure to have your dog on a front-connecting harness and a leash if you are practicing this outside.

WALKING NICELY ON LEASH AND *HEEL*

Loose leash walking is a means of keeping your dog nearby as you go for walks. He can sniff, meander, relieve himself, and play. This is also important because a dog who pulls on leash is difficult to control and poses a danger to himself and the person walking him. You will find that your independent-minded Beagle can learn to walk nicely and heel if you have persistence and patience. When heeling, however, he should be right at your side paying attention to you. You should have two different cues for these requirements so that your dog does not become confused.

How to Teach the *Heel*

Teaching the *heel* command first will help with teaching walking nicely on leash, or loose-leash walking, later on. You can use your targeting techniques for the *heel* and behavior shaping for the loose-leash walking.

1. Begin by calling your dog to come and sit at your left side. Have him face the same direction as you.
2. Next, hold a treat in your right hand and put it in front of your dog's nose.
3. With your dog focused on the treat, step forward with your left foot. As your dog follows, praise and reward him. Begin with only a couple steps, and gradually increase the number of steps you take as your Beagle follows through correctly. When you stop moving, use a *sit* cue, such as moving the treat over his head, between his eyes. This will enable you to reward him without losing his attention.
4. When you can move forward at least ten steps, incorporate some turns, and begin to change your pace a bit. Always stop frequently to have your dog sit and earn rewards. Also praise him as he moves with you to encourage the behavior.
5. You can begin to use a verbal command, such as "Heel" or "Let's

PUPPY POINTER

Young Beagles learn quickly but do not have a long attention span. You will be far more productive working with your pup for five or ten minutes at a time, several times each day, than trying to do so for 20 or 30 minutes in one session a day. This keeps your pup interested, coming back for more, and constantly trying to earn rewards instead of running to hide when he sees you coming with his leash.

Also, young Beagles have the most difficulty with learning the *stay* command. It is tough to keep their little bottoms in one place for any length of time. Continue to work on other commands such as *sit, down, come*, and *heel*, while slowly shaping the *stay* behavior by mere seconds, instead of minutes.

go," when your Beagle understands how to follow along with you and maintains focus on you. Eventually, you will be able to remove the constant targeting with a treat and transfer to rewarding your Beagle for good behavior with verbal praise instead. It will be far easier to make this transition if you offer lots of praise as he performs.

6. When you are done with heeling and having your dog perform other behaviors such as *sit, down*, and *stay*, release him from having to concentrate by giving him a release word, such as, "okay," break," or "free." This lets him know that he can stop performing the behavior. It helps to offer a gentle tap or petting as a reward as you say this.

How to Teach Walking Nicely on Leash

Now you are ready to begin teaching walking nicely on leash, or loose-leash walking.

1. Begin by working on the heel exercise, using a long leash at least 15 feet (5 m) in length, then release your dog from work by petting him.
2. Next, with your dog still on leash, move forward a few steps. If your dog follows you, praise and reward him.
3. Take a few moments to allow your dog to become otherwise engaged, such as sniffing the ground. Take a few more steps forward.
4. If your dog immediately runs to catch up, praise and reward him. If not, call him to come and sit, then praise and reward him.
5. Continue moving forward, repeating these steps frequently until your dog is paying attention to you enough to remain nearby as you move.
6. Gradually allow more space between you and your dog, letting him follow along nearby as he sniffs and enjoys his walk.

You can use the loose-leash walking cue while walking, hiking, or allowing your Beagle a chance to explore and be himself. However, when you have a distinct destination in mind, such as heading home, or going directly to a potty area, use the heeling cues so that you can attain your goal without any misunderstanding.

FINDING A PROFESSIONAL TRAINER

The best means of finding a professional trainer is to ask your veterinarian. Most likely, she has established a professional relationship with one in the area and has vetted out their methods and credentials.

However, should this not be the case, you can easily find one through the websites of these training organizations:
• The Association of Pet Dog Trainers: www.apdt.com

• The International Association of Canine Professionals:
www.canineprofessionals.com

Their websites list ways of choosing the right trainer for you and your situation, so read them thoroughly to avoid mistakes.

You can also ask friends and neighbors who have had good experiences with their trainers for a referral. If these options are not available to you, the Internet may be a good way to do some research. Using the search words "dog trainer," "pet trainer," or "canine trainer," along with your locale, in the search engines will usually net you many options.

To be sure you obtain professional help from someone who uses positive training techniques, thoroughly read their websites and also contact them to ask questions about how they train and if they are experienced working with Beagles. Most trainers will strive to earn your trust and business, but the only sure means of knowing that you are choosing a good trainer is through credentials, recommendations, and actually watching that person at work by attending a class. If you are comfortable with the trainer's techniques and achievements, then it is likely you will have a successful relationship and learn how to properly train your dog.

Once your dog learns all his obedience commands, there's no limit to what you can do together.

Beagles are not the easiest dogs to work with and will require much patience, understanding, and persistence. A trainer who tries to force a dog into acquiescence will not be as successful as one who guides, communicates, and uses positive methods to shape appropriate behavior. Moreover, the trainer must be an instructor with whom you are comfortable and who can communicate clearly and give you proper training skills because you are the one who will be living with and caring for your dog.

SOLVING PROBLEMS WITH YOUR BEAGLE

Just as with human children, Beagles must be taught how to behave, or they will not learn to perform appropriate behaviors as they mature. Your dog will not know your house rules or how to achieve positive results unless you train him. You need to guide him, direct his behavior patterns, and reward him whenever he behaves correctly—and do so in a timely manner to reinforce desired behaviors.

WHAT IS A PROBLEM BEHAVIOR?

A Beagle's behavior, like that of many dogs, tends to be problematic if he's not taught appropriate boundaries. This is not because Beagles are malicious; it is just that their nature—their normal canine instinct—directs their actions in ways that suit their basic needs and the jobs they were bred to do. They are scenthounds originally bred for long days of hunting and alerting to game. Therefore, it's up to you to redesign your Beagle's instincts in order to teach him to be a good canine citizen who is well-behaved in his home and in his community. Dogs love nothing better than to please us, so all your dog will need for accomplishing this is consistent positive training, time, and patience.

To deal with problem behaviors effectively, however, we must first understand that many of the behaviors people consider to be inappropriate are just normal behaviors for dogs—they do what comes naturally and makes sense to them in a given situation. But anything a dog does that is inconvenient, destructive, annoying, or dangerous is problematic for us because our canine companions live in our world, and we expect them to play by our rules. Once you understand what your dog is trying to communicate to you, though, you can successfully redirect unwanted behaviors toward acceptable ones.

DEALING WITH PROBLEM BEHAVIORS

As a general rule, begin training your dog the moment he enters your life. He should earn everything. There is a saying, "Nothing in life is free." Do you not have to work for a living? Rarely are wild animals able to lie around all day and still have shelter, food, and territory. Your dog may not be living in the wild, but he will be far better adjusted to living in your home if he learns how to earn his life rewards: food, treats, toys, and affection. This will keep him happy and less likely to initiate inappropriate behavior patterns or develop troubling neuroses.

To train your dog in this manner, you will need to establish default behaviors—this means that your dog must learn to perform a specific behavior prior to receiving things he wants, such as his meals or attention of any sort. A great default behavior is the *sit*. For example, your Beagle will have to sit as you put

down his food dish and wait before he can begin to eat, or he will have to sit for attention instead of jumping up on you. Your dog can also learn to sit prior to having his leash put on before going for walks. Should you live in a high-traffic area, your dog can learn to sit automatically before crossing the street. Default behaviors will teach your dog to control his natural urges to become excited and out of control in most situations, reverting instead to sitting because this behavior earns him the life rewards he desires.

Just as your Beagle will be trying hard to earn everything, so should you be aware of all that he does correctly. Catching him doing the right thing will go a long way toward reinforcing all his positive efforts. Be certain to praise and reward the moment he behaves in the manner

Once the root causes of problem behaviors are identified, they can usually be controlled or eliminated. Most are caused by boredom, lack of sufficient exercise, stress, or fear.

you want so that he will strive to repeat it, eventually becoming consistent. This type of redirection keeps your relationship positive. The clearer your communication, the faster your dog will learn and the fewer problem behaviors will occur. And you can count on some popping up as your Beagle goes from puppy to adolescent and on into adulthood.

PROBLEM BEHAVIORS IN ADULT DOGS

While all of this is great when working with a young dog who has not yet learned all the house rules, there are many older Beagles who engage in well-established inappropriate behaviors through lack of proper training. You will need to address this by teaching appropriate substitute behaviors and continuing to manage them in order to maintain a good relationship with your older dog.

If you adopt your adult Beagle from a shelter or Beagle rescue, you may need to address many behavior problems that have been well established in the dog's behavioral repertoire. While most are learned behaviors, some are self-rewarding and will be difficult to redirect. A sample of a self-rewarding behavior is jumping up. Beagles love to jump about. Even if they do not attain the attention they crave by jumping on you, they are still likely to touch you, which is rewarding to them. Barking is another self-rewarding behavior. Beagles love to bark, so redirecting an excessively barking Beagle will not be easy. You must be patient!

Be consistent in your house rules and training. The basic premise behind successful positive training is to reward the behaviors that you like, while ignoring (if possible) behaviors you don't like. In other words, praise and reward your Beagle when he does the right thing and avoid offering any semblance of a reward when he does something inappropriate. As with all training, keep sessions short, positive, and fun. In time, your dog will learn what is expected of him, and you'll both be happier for it.

AGGRESSION

It is rare for a Beagle to display aggression. This is not generally a dominant or territorial breed. There might be some situations, though, in which your Beagle is in pain or in which he has learned to be possessive of food, toys, or even his human companions. These are cases where the behavior will need to be retrained.

MANAGEMENT

The first step in dealing with aggressive behavior is to take your dog to your veterinarian. A sudden case of aggression can indicate a health issue. A medical exam will either rule out or uncover the root cause of the behavior.

Should your Beagle receive a clean bill of health, review his diet to be certain he is receiving the appropriate amount of nutrients and proteins. Often a sudden food reaction or lack of required minerals and vitamins can trigger a behavioral abnormality.

Some Beagles can be assertive with siblings or playmates. If this occurs, you will always need to supervise them when they are together and quickly redirect aggressive behavior. For example, if play becomes too rough, call your dog to come to you. Reward him when he arrives so that he will be more likely to always come to you when he feels upset or gets into a bad situation. A well-trained Beagle can easily be calmed down and redirected. Getting upset will only make matters worse, and make the dog more assertive as emotions run high.

Should your dog show signs

If you think your dog may be showing signs of aggressive behavior but you're not sure, consult a professional behaviorist or trainer. These dogs are engaged in defensive play.

of dangerous aggression such as growling, snarling, deep barking, or lunging, contact a professional dog trainer or pet behaviorist right away. Only a knowledgeable professional can discern the reason for the behavior and instruct you in how to properly cure and/or manage this type of dangerous behavior.

BARKING

Beagles bark. If not taught otherwise, they will bark excessively. Whether barking at an approaching animal, person, or butterfly, Beagles love to hear the sound of their own voice. After all, one of their most historically useful characteristics is their bray, which notifies their human hunting companions of game. It would not be fair to your Beagle to punish him for doing what is entirely natural deep down in his genetic composition. However, you can modify and manage his barking to some extent.

MANAGEMENT

If you have a young Beagle, remain with him when he is outdoors. Exercise in the yard is great, but there are numerous inappropriate behaviors that will worsen if you do not observe and redirect them immediately and consistently. For Beagles, barking is one of these behaviors.

When your pup begins to bark at something, redirect his attention to a toy. The toy should be something that moves or tastes good; otherwise, barking will still be far more attractive to him. Interactive games are best because your Beagle would prefer to play with you. You can play fetch, chase, or tug. In general, keep your little guy busy so that he believes that your games are more fun than barking.

If you have an older dog that you've adopted, you can try the same techniques used with a pup, but this may not always be successful because your older dog has already learned how fulfilling it can be to bark. One means of managing your older Beagle's excessive barking is to teach him to do it on cue. Once he learns to bark when asked to do so, you can then teach him when not to bark. This is done first through facilitation of the bark by using a verbal and/or visual cue on the occasions when your dog will be permitted to bark, such as when someone comes to the door or yard gate.

As your Beagle barks, use a visual cue, such as putting your hand behind your ear with the palm out, as you say, "Speak." Praise and reward him when he speaks (barks) on cue. Because Beagles are quick to recognize when a behavior is rewarding, and because they love to bark anyway, your dog will respond well to this command. Never yell or lose your temper if your dog doesn't respond appropriately. Every dog learns at his own pace.

When your dog successfully barks on cue, teach him when to stop barking. As he's barking, turn your back to him and give the verbal cue "Quiet." The moment he is quiet, reward him. Gradually increase the amount of time your dog must be quiet prior to rewarding him. Do this in very small steps or he will not fully understand what you want. For example, begin with a three-second "Quiet." When he's successful with that period of time, go to a five-second "Quiet." If you reach a minute or two, and he suddenly seems to not understand, return to a time for which he was reliable. This is termed "regress to progress."

If your dog barks excessively when left alone, he is likely bored and lonely.

You can further this training by teaching your Beagle "Inside voice," "Outside voice," and "Sneeze." Merely offer a cue for the behavior and reward the exact moment he offers it. Within a couple repetitions, your Beagle will have a full vocal repertoire. Just make certain to reward his vocalizations only when they are requested.

DESTRUCTIVE CHEWING

All dogs will chew, especially as young pups. Between teething, high-energy levels, and lack of constant observation in order to redirect the behavior, you can count on your Beagle chewing and damaging some of your possessions. The key is to make certain he chews his toys and not household items.

Older Beagles are unlikely to be destructive chewers, unless they have separation anxiety. This disorder is not common in Beagles because they tend to have independent personalities unlike most retrievers or herding breeds. However, if bored, they also can be destructive to some extent.

MANAGEMENT

The best means of preventing destructive chewing is to make certain that your dog receives plenty of exercise. A tired Beagle is less likely to expend energy by chewing the wrong things. Exercise also stimulates his mind so he will be less bored. A tired, sleeping hound is a well-behaved hound.

Another way to ensure that your Beagle pup does not chew on the wrong items is to provide him with a variety of appropriate chew toys. Rotating his toys every day or two will help maintain his interest in them. If you are not tripping over toys in your pup's play area, there are likely not enough of them because you will need to reach one quickly to redirect his attentions should he begin to chew a table leg. Wiggle or drag the toy to further increase his enthusiasm for it; moving "prey" is more attractive than the convenient tree branch disguised as a table leg.

Should you wish to occupy your Beagle for a while, try offering him an interactive or treat-filled toy. An interactive toy is something that he must move around or pull apart in order to be rewarded with food or several chews. A treat-filled toy is something that offers a means of holding or containing kibble, peanut butter, cheese, or biscuits, which a dog must work at to consume. A hollow beef shank bone, filled with creamed vegetables or cheese and then frozen is a great treat for a teething puppy.

DIGGING

All dogs dig. Beagles are hunting dogs, so they will definitely dig when catching the scent of something interesting. Unfortunately, the digging might occur in the wrong place, for example in your boxwood or perennial flower beds. Beagles do not understand the difference between digging in the woods and rearranging your landscaping.

MANAGEMENT

Once again, you will need to observe and direct your dog while he is in your yard. When he begins to dig in the wrong place, coax him to an area set aside just for his digging enjoyment. If you cannot watch your dog, do not allow him freedom in the garden. You should create a space just for your Beagle—one where he can dig to his heart's content.

A means of detracting your dog from digging in inappropriate areas is to fill the holes he makes with his own feces. Few dogs like to dig near their own droppings.

This may not be suitable if you have a small yard, so another means of applying a scent that will detract him from digging in the area is to pour vinegar around the hole. It is a strong odor that most dogs, especially those with a sensitive nose like your Beagle, will avoid.

HOUSE SOILING

Few dogs will naturally soil their dens. If your Beagle is soiling in the house, it means he has not learned that his den comprises more space. When you have clearly established his potty area, it is unlikely that he will soil elsewhere. However, if you do not consistently adhere to his schedule, he might soil in a room in which he does not spend much time. In essence, he is treating it as a space outside of his den area. Routine and consistency are tantamount in preventing house-soiling accidents.

MANAGEMENT

Dogs who do not understand when and where to potty will often do so anywhere. To teach your dog that his relief area is outside, you will need to consistently guide him and make certain that you abide by a specific potty schedule. Also, he must be safely contained when you cannot watch him; this means crate confinement. However, do not confine your dog in a crate for long hours. That is not fair to him. Often doggy daycare can be helpful for this and other problems caused by changes in your schedule that may affect your dog's potty routine, as well as elimination problems that may be caused by anxiety or a health condition. At doggy daycare, your Beagle will be walked and receive ample

BE AWARE!

You can often prevent your Beagle from begging at the table by never offering him food while you are seated and eating a meal. This advice is the same for counter-surfing behaviors. Never feed your dog from the counter station while you are preparing meals.

Teach your Beagle that the only places he receives food are from his dish or from your hand while training. To accomplish and reinforce this, all you need to do is be consistent—never give him food in any other situation or allow others to do so.

Dogs jump up because they are seeking attention. One way to train your Beagle not to jump up is to completely ignore him when he does so.

exercise, socialization, and some behavior guidance.

Sometimes your dog may have an accident when it is not really his fault. He came to tell you that he needed to go potty, but you ignored him. This often happens when pet owners do not recognize the "potty dance." In young Beagles, this may be whimpering, pacing, sniffing, or walking in a tight circle. In older dogs, it may be indicated by coming near you, staring at you, or running to the door and back to you. Other dogs merely sit at the door anxiously waiting. If you're occupied, you will miss these signals.

You can improve your dog's track record by teaching him to potty on command. This way, you can be certain he has emptied prior to returning to the house. Keep in mind, however, that male dogs may need to go more than once, especially if not neutered by adulthood.

Begin the association by giving your dog a specific cue word, such as "potty" or "empty," the moment you take him to his potty spot first thing in the morning. He is sure to potty at that time, increasing the success rate of association. The moment he is finished, reward him. Repeat this procedure each time you take your dog to his potty area.

There may be times when your dog becomes more interested in scenting than in relieving himself. Standing outside and repeating his potty cue over and over will get old quickly and will set back his housetraining progress. When this occurs, return your Beagle to his crate and try again in about 20 minutes. Your dog will soon learn to potty when he hears the cue word because it is far more rewarding to receive a food treat than to have to return to bed.

JUMPING UP

Beagles are happy, enthusiastic dogs. They love to include their humans in their games and will often initiate this by jumping up. While they have a natural proclivity toward this behavior, it is only through reinforcement that it becomes a real problem. The reinforcement comes from your reaction when your dog jumps on you. Do you touch him? Look at him and speak to him? All these responses are rewards to your dog. Even more rewarding is when you attempt to push him away; then it becomes a really fun game.

MANAGEMENT

The best means of teaching your dog to stop an annoying behavior is to stop offering rewards for it. The next time your Beagle tries to jump up on you, turn away from him. Don't look at him, speak to him, or touch him. On the contrary, when your dog sits and waits for your attention, lavish him with tons of praise and affection. This will teach him an alternative means of garnering attention—sitting for it.

Some Beagles will continually jump up on you and on others no matter how much you try to ignore them. For these dogs, the mere act of jumping is such a great reward that they have no wish to learn alternative attention-seeking behavior. If this is the case with your dog, enlist the aid of a professional dog trainer who will discern the reasons for your dog's inappropriate behavior and help you redirect him in a positive manner.

NIPPING

Most puppies will nip, whether in play or in exploration. Dogs use their mouths as we use our hands. They take, hold, pull, and explore. A human toddler uses her hands to explore as well—for example, to bring items to her mouth to taste. Dogs go straight for the grab and taste.

Punishing your dog for this behavior would not be fair because it is a natural tendency. However, it's important that he learn that he should never use his teeth on his human guardians, not even during play. You can redirect your dog toward more appropriate interactions by indicating to him that he is not allowed to nip or nibble by saying (not yelling) "No" or by introducing him to the "Game over" technique.

MANAGEMENT

When your Beagle puts his mouth on you, stop interacting with him. Say "No" in a low tone or say "Game over." Stop all contact with him (which is a correction cue). If he stops and sits calmly, reengage with him. Should you feel his teeth again, move away and stop all contact as you use your correction cue. Because Beagles crave attention and play, your dog will quickly learn that nipping is not acceptable.

FINDING PROFESSIONAL HELP

Should you encounter an unexplainable behavior, or have difficulty in redirecting your Beagle into appropriate behavior, obtain the council of a professional trainer or behaviorist. In fact, to prevent the majority of inappropriate behaviors that you may encounter as your pup matures, consider enrolling your dog in obedience classes. This will give you the tools and knowledge you need for properly guiding your dog in the right direction.

Dog Tale

As dogs get older, they often develop insecurities, and, sometimes, possessive behaviors. When one of my dogs was 9 years old, she would gather as many toys as she could when the other dogs were not in the room, take them to a corner, and lay on top of them. When another dog came near, she would growl at them and show her teeth. As she did this, she quivered all over.

Observing this abnormal behavior, I took her to the veterinarian for a complete physical. We discovered she suffered from progressive spondylosis, which causes bone spurs along her vertebrae. She had become protective of herself as any jostling with her pack mates was painful. Also, her ability to protect herself was diminishing, so she took a proactive stance by being territorial. At this point, I had to separate her from the other dogs so that she would not incite aggression or be hurt by rough canine play.

While these types of behaviors can often be due to failing health, they also can stem from allowing your dog to gradually assert himself at the wrong times. To keep your older Beagle calmer and happier, remain consistent and positive in his training throughout his life, especially when he tests your authority. An older dog might need refresher training, or merely a return to some basic obedience routines. Once involved in your life again and engaged in activities that both stimulate his mind and encourage him to be successful, the unwanted or attention-seeking behavior will extinguish and you will once again have a happy, well-behaved dog.

You can obtain a list of professional trainers from the Association of Pet Dog Trainers (APDT) at 800-738-3647 (PET-DOGS) or through their website at www.apdt.com. Another reliable source for information is the International Association of Canine Professionals (IACP) website at www.canineprofessionals.com.

For more serious problems, you may want to enlist the services of an animal behaviorist. You can obtain information from The International Association of Animal Behavior Consultants (IAABC) at 484-843-1091 or by visiting their website at www.iaabc.org. This online resource features many informative articles as well as a list of behaviorists who are located in your area.

Your veterinarian may also be able to recommend a trainer or behaviorist. Often veterinarians will have spoken with and reviewed the credentials of dog trainers in your area and will be able to advise you on, and provide contact information for, someone who might best help you with your particular canine problem.

ACTIVITIES WITH
YOUR BEAGLE

Beagles are great pets and lots of fun. They love activity and a good challenge. There are many sports and activities in which you and your Beagle can team up and participate. Earning titles and certificates of achievement are great goals that involve lots of positive interaction with your dog. But just tossing a ball around in the yard, going for long walks, traveling together, or doing therapy work can be rewarding, too.

SPORTS AND ACTIVITIES

Versatile, energetic dogs, Beagles learn easily if trained using patience and persistence as well as positive methods. The more rewarding an activity is for your Beagle, the more he will excel.

The first goal of any pet owner should be to help his dog obtain one of the American Kennel Club (AKC) training certificates, which are offered for puppies and adults. The AKC training programs are also a good stepping stone for other fun events such as agility, conformation, field trials, obedience, rally, and the most helpful and fulfilling job of therapy dog.

The Canine Good Citizen (CGC) test encourages owners to foster and encourage good manners in their dogs.

In order to participate in these activities, your Beagle will need to learn how to travel well and behave in new environments. This involves making sure your dog has impeccable manners, which includes basic on- and off- leash training skills, and that he is secure in his acceptance of new places and experiences. This also requires effort on your part. For pet-friendly lodging and parks to remain pet friendly, it is your responsibility to clean up after your dog and make certain he makes a good impression on all who meet him.

CANINE GOOD CITIZEN PROGRAM

The AKC promotes good care and training of dogs by offering several certification programs that reflect how well dog owners follow through with their responsibilities. The first level of achievement is the Socialization, Training, Activity, Responsibility Puppy (S.T.A.R. Puppy) program. If you have children who wish to be involved with the care and training of your Beagle, this is a great place to begin the relationship in a positive manner. More information about this program can be obtained on the AKC's website, or at www.akc.org/pdfs/starpuppy/brochure.pdf.

The next level of achievement to attain is the Canine Good Citizen (CGC) program, which will prepare your dog for behaving at home, in his community, and when traveling. All dogs should earn this certificate because it requires that they, and their people, go through training classes to learn proper handling techniques and some essential basic commands.

Canine Good Citizen Test

Generally, this test is designed to ensure that dogs can behave while being handled and greeted by strangers. It also ensures that dogs can behave when confronted with distractions and when briefly left alone.

There are ten parts to the CGC test. They are as follows:

1. Accepting a friendly stranger (the dog allows someone to come near and speak to his handler without reacting with excitement or aggression).
2. Sitting politely while being petted by a stranger.
3. Permitting examination and grooming (this will prepare your dog for handling by a veterinarian, groomer, etc.).
4. Ability to walk with you on a loose leash, preferably without any pulling.
5. Walking calmly through a crowd (this is especially important if you intend to take your dog with you to your children's sporting events, or if you live in an urban area where your dog must walk a block or more to reach his play area).
6. Performing a *sit* and *down-stay* (these are important skills for all dogs because they should sit prior to crossing streets and going through doors or gates).
7. Coming when called (although difficult for the Beagle who prefers to follow a scent rather than listening, this command is important in every situation).
8. Behaving around other dogs (this is a tough one because most Beagles love to greet other dogs).
9. Behaving around distractions (this includes joggers, bicyclists, rolling balls, dropped objects, and more).
10. Supervised separation (this will check for separation anxiety).

The best means of accomplishing these goals is to participate in obedience classes, specifically those that address these achievements. There are dog clubs and other training groups that offer CGC classes for dogs who have completed prior basic training classes.

AGILITY

As fun to watch as it is to compete in, agility involves a combination of jumping, running, and handling direction through a series of obstacles on a timed course. You will need to be as conditioned as your Beagle because you will have to move through the course quickly and guide your dog concisely.

Beagles are not known for speed, but they can traverse any obstacle. If in good condition, they also have good stamina. They are hunting dogs who have been bred to work until the sun goes down.

Despite not having the speed to compete, your dog can still earn titles through a successful course completion. You will need only to keep his nose pointed forward instead of downward—a tough thing for Beagles who love to sniff. Positive reinforcement training can teach him to be attentive in anticipation of the rewards he will earn.

You can obtain more information about agility at the following websites:
• American Kennel Club: www.akc.org/events/agility/
• United States Dog Agility Association: www.usdaa.com/
• The Dog Owner's Guide: www.canismajor.com

CONFORMATION

Conformation events are geared toward improving the breed as defined by the standard of excellence for that breed. Hence, only those dogs who closely resemble the characteristics and colors delineated in the breed standard participate in bench shows. Most of these dogs are shown by professional handlers who fully understand how to present them in their best light. Rarely does a novice handler fare well unless a dog is so outstanding that poor presentation does not deter from his overall qualities and success in the show ring.

Essentially, conformation showing is similar to a beauty contest, though attitude also plays a big part. Uno, the Beagle who won at Westminster in 2008, received his Best in Show title not just due to his great conformation and superior conditioning but also due to his outgoing, fun personality, which sparkled "Look at me" in neon.

If you plan on showing your Beagle in conformation, be certain to take classes on proper grooming and presentation, and go to many shows, observing how the winning dogs are presented. You would also benefit from experience at local matches and, when ready, local dog shows. Each show will teach you something, and in the show ring, experience is everything.

A Beagle who earns the title Champion (CH) after his name is one who is worthy of being bred because he will maintain breed standards, if not also improve the breed's appearance. However, because Beagles were originally bred to hunt, having hunting titles after their names is equally appealing in enhancing the overall performance of their offspring.

FIELD TRIALS

Due to the Beagle's natural ability to scent, this breed excels in tracking activities. Best of all, they can move ahead of their handlers and lead the way, not having to be attentive to anything other than the trail.

In a conformation show, a dog is evaluated on how closely he conforms to the breed standard.

There are several ways to compete in Beagle Field Trials: as part of a brace (two or three dogs), small pack, large pack, and gundog brace. There are also hunt tests.

The Brace event judges how well two dogs work as a team to track down prey, in this case a rabbit. The Small Pack event consists of seven dogs who are judged on how well they track and pursue a rabbit. The Large Pack event consists of 22 dogs who must run after a rabbit scent for upwards of three hours in an open competition in which they earn points toward Field Trial Championships. The Gundog Brace event consists of two to three Beagles who are judged on finding their own rabbit trail, tracking down and chasing the rabbit, and handling the sound of gunfire. Hunt Tests consist of four dogs who are paired and must find their own rabbit trail and track the rabbit. They are evaluated on how well they search for game. A dog who passes this test earns a Master Hunter (MH) after his name.

You can obtain more information about these Field Trial events at the AKC's website at www.akc.org/events/field_trials/beagles.

OBEDIENCE

Obedience trials have three levels—novice, open, and utility—with numerous championship titles beyond these, inviting dog/handler teams to continually train and compete.

At the novice level, exercises are done both on and off leash. Your dog will need to perform *heel, sit/stay, down/stay, come, finish,* and *stand.* Variation exercises include a figure-8 at the *heel* and long-distance *stays* with dogs on either side. At the open level, your dog will need to do all exercises off leash. This level also includes retrieving, jumping, and out-of-sight *stays.* The utility level is extremely challenging because the dog must discern the difference between your scent and that of another person during a scent-discrimination exercise. He will also need to perform a *go out,* in which he follows your directions for which jump to go over and which scented glove to pick up. This level requires a lot of concentration, which is really not the Beagle's forte. However, if you put in enough effort, your dog can accomplish anything.

Challenging and requiring lots of preparation, obedience trials separate the dog/handler teams who are prepared from those who are not. This type of activity requires more dedication to training and handling than most of the other events. Your dog must learn absolute concentration on his handler while working off leash among incredible distractions. Moreover, there will not be constant action as in other sports such as agility and rally. Maintaining attention when stationary can prove difficult.

RALLY

The sport of rally is fun for the entire team. Beagles love this because they are constantly moving and being challenged at each station. A rally course is designed by a judge and consists of 15 to 22 stations, each with a different exercise. The course encompasses exercises used in other types of competition, such as obedience and agility. From circles, jumps, and complicated maneuvers to simple turns and stops, rally is similar to freestyle, which is "dancing" with your dog, though the handler does not have to choreograph the performance.

Rally requires the dog to be well trained on and off leash in all phases of obedience. This includes *heel, sit-stay, down-stay, come, finish* (return to heel position at both the left and right), *stand-stay*, and more. Most of all, this event requires the handler to fully understand and recognize the station signs and know how to guide her dog into the best performance possible.

A Beagle who participates in activities is a happier and healthier pet.

Many dog-training clubs offer classes in this activity. Whether or not you wish to compete, it is lots of fun to learn and practice. This will exercise your Beagle's mind and body sufficiently to tire him out for a couple hours.

You can obtain more information about this activity at the following websites:
• Rally Obedience: www.rallyobedience.com
• American Kennel Club: www.akcrallyobedience.com and www.akc.org/rules/

THERAPY WORK

This is where Beagles shine. They love attention, and people who see their cute face and wagging tail will be happy to offer it. Once your Beagle is socialized and well trained, you can begin to share his great personality and love of everyone with those who really need to feel this affection—children, the elderly, and those who are hospitalized. Nothing helps the healing process better than an animal showing affection. The mere action of stroking a dog has been shown to have great therapeutic properties.

There are several organizations dedicated to preparing and guiding pets through the process of becoming effective therapy dogs. The Delta Society and Therapy Dogs International are two highly respected organizations. You can obtain more information via their websites at www.deltasociety.com and www.tdi.org, respectively.

Your Beagle must be able to pass the CGC test, which was discussed earlier in this chapter, as well as learn how to perform well in a variety of environments with myriad distractions. This is important because you don't want your dog to injure someone who is weak or ill, despite his good intentions.

Should you wish to train your Beagle to become a therapy dog, make certain that you have the time to dedicate to consistently taking your dog to his job. People begin to look forward to visits with their doggy therapists. Disappointment from a no-show can have adverse effects on someone who is mentally challenged or very ill. Your Beagle might also be depressed to not visit with his friends.

TRAVELING WITH YOUR DOG

Beagles love adventure. Going for a car ride to the park or just to the store is cause for excitement. Here are some suggestions on how to keep the experience positive and safe for your dog.

RIDING IN CARS WITH BEAGLES

Your first priority when your Beagle rides along with you in the car is safety and appropriate behavior. Your second priority is making sure that the conditions in your car do not adversely affect your dog, such as the temperature being too hot or too cold, and having any supplies he may need during travel.

Safety

It's never a good idea to allow your Beagle freedom to move around in the car. Besides being a distraction to you, it is also dangerous for him. If you stop or turn suddenly, your dog can be thrown about and injured. Containment of some sort will ensure that he remains safe and enjoys each travel experience. A crate is a reliable means of securing your dog inside your vehicle, as is a seat belt, provided the seat belt does not offer him too much freedom of movement. Booster seats with seat belts are generally safe as well.

Your Beagle also should learn how to travel quietly. The last thing you need while driving is a dog who is barking excessively and pawing at the upholstery. Review your obedience training techniques (see Chapter 7), and practice them in the car to teach your dog that you expect him to behave wherever you go.

Travel Needs

Always have some water and a water dish in the car, along with cleaning supplies, such as paper towels, premoistened wipes, and plastic bags. Also, your dog should wear a collar with an identification tag that shows your contact information, along with his rabies tag. And if your Beagle has earned his CGC certificate, by all means advertise that he is a good citizen by having him wear the tag. Of course, it goes without saying that your dog should always be on leash when accompanying you at your various destinations.

Temperature Conditions

Generally, it would be a good idea to take your dog with you only when he can participate in whatever it is

Dog Tale

In the three decades that I have been providing animals for feature films, television, and advertising, Beagles have been frequently requested. They are the all-American dog, able to perform complicated behaviors amid numerous distractions for long periods of time. They good naturedly accept the presence of strangers and other animals with an exuberant greeting and wagging tail.

Should you have an interest in your Beagle working in the entertainment industry, contact the film commission in your state to get a listing of agents in your region. Animal actor agents often use the talents of pet Beagles because they are intelligent, charming, and always ready for some fun.

you are going to do, say picking up the kids at school or picking up some take-out, in which case, he would be left alone in the car for only a brief period of time.

The ambient temperature inside your car will make all the difference on where you are able to go with your Beagle. For example, if you are planning a trip to the grocery store and must leave your dog alone in the car for more than 5 minutes, you should reconsider allowing him to tag along. If it is summer, or hotter than 60°F (16°C), and you are leaving him just for a few minutes, make sure your dog has adequate ventilation and cool water. Never park your car and keep the windows all the way up, even in cold weather, as the lack of ventilation can be dangerous. Leaving the windows down is also dangerous because your dog can jump out and become lost, or he may be stolen.

Planning Ahead

Wherever you plan on going, check in advance to be sure your destination is pet-friendly, and also check out the proximity of the closest 24-hour veterinary clinics in case of an emergency. Take copies of your dog's veterinary records along with you if you are going to be away on an extended trip.

Also, don't give your dog a heavy meal just before a long car trip because the excitement and motion can sometimes upset his stomach. A light meal two to

BE AWARE!

Senior dogs still love to participate in family activities. Be sure that you don't forget your best friend when you consider family events and travel. Should you have any qualms about what your old dog can handle, consult with your veterinarian. Your dog may have special food or medication considerations, not to mention mobility issues.

When traveling by car with a senior dog, a ramp might be a convenient means of letting him in and out of the vehicle. Some senior dogs do not appreciate being lifted because it can be painful, so having an easy way to enter and exit on their own will prevent unnecessary pain and stress.

Many senior dogs require more water and more frequent relief opportunities. Be sure to take this into consideration by offering your old guy water more often and finding a place to walk him every few hours, especially if you are on a long trip.

Because air travel can be very stressful on any dog, it is not a great idea to subject your senior to this if you can make other arrangements. He might be far happier and remain healthier if you are able to arrange for a pet sitter or keep him at a comfortable pet resort where he will receive good care and observation.

three hours before you leave, with a little bit of water throughout the time you travel, will help keep his stomach settled. Good preparation ensures that both you and your dog will travel comfortably and safely.

FLYING ACES

Flying with your dog also requires a lot of preparation. Because Beagles are too large to fit beneath an airline seat, they must travel crated in the cargo area. This area is normally temperature controlled, but the tarmac is not. It is wise not to have your dog travel by air during extreme temperatures, such as above 80°F (27°C) and below 32°F (0°C). While most Beagles can acclimate very well to these temperature extremes, the stress of air travel will lower their resistance to illness and diminish their ability to adjust to these temperatures.

If your Beagle is less than 8 weeks of age, or has a respiratory illness, he should not travel by air. The stress of the situation would be far too dangerous. Also, if you will have connecting flights or your dog has to remain in his crate for more than six hours, it will be difficult for him to contain his urine. When you make your flight plans, take into consideration prior to the flight the amount of time your dog must be in his crate as well as the additional time it will take to unload and shuttle him to you in the terminal.

Here is a checklist of preparations to make prior to flying with your dog:

- Check out the airline's requirements prior to making reservations. Rules and regulations are prone to sudden change without notification to passengers. Something as simple as an overbooked flight, leaving you behind as your dog travels ahead of you, can be extremely problematic.
- Purchase an airline-approved travel crate. These are constructed of hard plastic, with a metal mesh door and venting on the sides. This type of crate will keep your dog safe from luggage or other items falling on him, as well as most flying particulate matter. Most dogs also feel safer when they are surrounded by something solid. Write down your dog's identification information on the crate, along with your contact information. Your cell phone number will also be most important.
- Place a secure water dish inside the crate. Something that fastens onto the door is fine, especially if it can be a water bottle, which will prevent total spillage when the crate is transported from terminal to tarmac and onto the plane via the conveyor. You should avoid offering food to your dog during the trip. However, you can offer him some comfort with a couple of safe chew toys and a comfortable bed.

The moment you have custody of your dog after the flight, clip on his leash and remove him from the crate. Take him directly to a relief area to stretch his legs. Once he is relaxed and comfortable, offer him some water and food.

Because your Beagle has keen senses, he will know if you are stressed and worried. If you are insecure, he will know this and react accordingly. Try to remain as positive, happy, and relaxed as possible so that he will not receive any unsettling emotion from you. He relies on you to keep him safe and to lead him, both at home and during your travels together.

RESOURCES

ASSOCIATIONS AND ORGANIZATIONS

BREED CLUBS

American Kennel Club (AKC)
5580 Centerview Drive
Raleigh, NC 27606
Telephone: (919) 233-9767
Fax: (919) 233-3627
E-Mail: info@akc.org
www.akc.org

The Beagle Club (UK)
www.thebeagleclub.org

Canadian Kennel Club (CKC)
89 Skyway Avenue, Suite 100
Etobicoke, Ontario M9W 6R4
Telephone: (416) 675-5511
Fax: (416) 675-6506
E-Mail: information@ckc.ca
www.ckc.ca

Federation Cynologique
Internationale (FCI)
Secretariat General de la FCI
Place Albert 1er, 13
B — 6530 Thuin
Belqique
www.fci.be

The Kennel Club
1 Clarges Street
London
W1J 8AB
Telephone: 0870 606 6750
Fax: 0207 518 1058
www.the-kennel-club.org.uk

National Beagle Club of America
http://clubs.akc.org/NBC

United Kennel Club (UKC)
100 E. Kilgore Road
Kalamazoo, MI 49002-5584
Telephone: (269) 343-9020
Fax: (269) 343-7037
E-Mail: pbickell@ukcdogs.com
www.ukcdogs.com

PET SITTERS

National Association of
Professional Pet Sitters
15000 Commerce Parkway, Suite C
Mt. Laurel, New Jersey 08054
Telephone: (856) 439-0324
Fax: (856) 439-0525
E-Mail: napps@ahint.com
www.petsitters.org

Pet Sitters International
201 East King Street
King, NC 27021-9161
Telephone: (336) 983-9222
Fax: (336) 983-5266
E-Mail: info@petsit.com
www.petsit.com

RESCUE ORGANIZATIONS AND ANIMAL WELFARE GROUPS

American Humane Association
(AHA)
63 Inverness Drive East
Englewood, CO 80112
Telephone: (303) 792-9900
Fax: 792-5333
www.americanhumane.org

American Society for the
Prevention of Cruelty to Animals
(ASPCA)
424 E. 92nd Street
New York, NY 10128-6804
Telephone: (212) 876-7700
www.aspca.org

Canadian Federation of Humane
Societies (CFHS)
102-30 Concourse Gate
Ottawa, ON K2E 7V7
Canada
Telephone: (888) 678-CFHS
Fax: (613)723-0252
E-mail: info@cfhs.ca
www.cfhs.ca

Royal Society for the Prevention
of Cruelty to Animals (RSPCA)
RSPCA Enquiries Service
Wilberforce Way, Southwater,
Horsham, West Sussex RH13 9RS
United Kingdom
Telephone: 0870 3335 999
Fax: 0870 7530 284
www.rspca.org.uk

SPORTS

North American Flyball
Association (NAFA)
1400 West Devon Avenue, #512
Chicago, IL 60660
Telephone/Fax: (800) 318-6312
E-mail: flyball@flyball.org
www.flyball.org

United States Dog Agility
Association (USDAA)
P.O. Box 850955
Richardson, TX 75085-0955
Telephone: (972) 487-2200
Fax: (972) 231-9700
E-mail: info@usdaa.com
www.usdaa.com

The World Canine Freestyle
Organization, Inc.
P.O. Box 350122
Brooklyn, NY 11235
Telephone: (718) 332-8336
Fax: (718) 646-2686
E-Mail: WCFODOGS@aol.com
www.worldcaninefreestyle.org

THERAPY

Delta Society Pet Partners
Program
875 124th Ave, NE, Suite 101
Bellevue, WA 98005
Telephone: (425) 679-5500
Fax: (425) 679-5539
E-Mail. info@DeltaSociety.org
www.deltasociety.org

Therapy Dogs International
88 Bartley Road
Flanders, NJ 07836
Telephone: (973) 252-9800
Fax: (973) 252-7171
E-Mail: tdi@gti.net
www.tdi-dog.org

TRAINING

Association of Pet Dog Trainers
(APDT)
150 Executive Center Drive Box 35
Greenville, SC 29615
Telephone: (800) PET-DOGS
Fax: (864) 331-0767
E-Mail: information@apdt.com
www.apdt.com

International Association of
Animal Behavior Consultants
(IAABC)
565 Callery Road
Cranberry Township, PA 16066
E-Mail: info@iaabc.org
www.iaabc.org

National Association of Dog
Obedience Instructors (NADOI)
PMB 369
729 Grapevine Hwy.
Hurst, TX 76054-2085
www.nadoi.org

VETERINARY AND HEALTH RESOURCES

Academy of Veterinary
Homeopathy (AVH)
P.O. Box 232282
Leucadia, CA 92023-2282
Telephone/Fax: (866) 652-1590
www.theavh.com/contact/index.
php

American Academy of Veterinary
Acupuncture (AAVA)
P.O. Box 1058
Glastonbury, CT 06033
Telephone: (860) 632-9911
Fax: (860) 659-8772
www.aava.org

American Animal Hospital
Association (AAHA)
12575 W. Bayaud Ave.
Lakewood, CO 80228
Telephone: (303) 986-2800
Fax: (303) 986-1700
E-Mail: info@aahanet.org
www.aahanet.org/index.cfm

American College of Veterinary
Internal Medicine (ACVIM)
1997 Wadsworth Blvd., Suite A
Lakewood, CO 80214-5293
Telephone: (800) 245-9081
Fax: (303) 231-0880
Email: ACVIM@ACVIM.org
www.acvim.org

American College of Veterinary
Ophthalmologists (ACVO)
P.O. Box 1311
Meridian, ID 83860
Telephone: (208) 466-7624
Fax: (208) 466-7693
E-Mail: office09@acvo.com
www.acvo.com

American Holistic Veterinary
Medical Association (AHVMA)
2218 Old Emmorton Road
Bel Air, MD 21015
Telephone: (410) 569-0795
Fax: (410) 569-2346
E-Mail: office@ahvma.org
www.ahvma.org

American Veterinary Medical
Association (AVMA)
1931 North Meacham Road, Suite
100
Schaumburg, IL 60173-4360
Telephone: (847) 925-8070
Fax: (847) 925-1329
E-Mail: avmainfo@avma.org
www.avma.org

ASPCA Animal Poison Control
Center
Telephone: (888) 426-4435
www.aspca.org

British Veterinary Association
(BVA)
7 Mansfield Street
London
W1G 9NQ
Telephone: 0207 636 6541
Fax: 0207 908 6349
E-Mail: bvahq@bva.co.uk
www.bva.co.uk

Canine Eye Registration
Foundation (CERF)
VMDB/CERF
1248 Lynn Hall
625 Harrison St.
Purdue University
W. Lafayette, IN 47907-2026
Telephone: (765) 494-8179
E-mail: CERF@vmdb.org
www.vmdb.org/cerf.html

Orthopedic Foundation for Animals (OFA)
2300 NE Nifong Blvd
Columbus, Missouri 65201-3806
Phone: (800) 442-0418
E-mail: chic@offa.org
www.offa.org

US Food and Drug Administration
Center for Veterinary Medicine (CVM)
7519 Standish Place
HFV-12
Rockville, MD 20855-0001
Telephone: (240) 276-9300
E-mail: ASKCVM@fda.hhs.gov
www.fda.gov/cvm/default.htm

Veterinary Pet Insurance
P.O. Box 2344
Brea, CA 92822-2344
Telephone: (800) USA-PETS
www.petinsurance.com

PUBLICATIONS
BOOKS
Anderson, Teoti. *The Super Simple Guide to Housetraining*. Neptune City: TFH Publications, 2004.

Anne, Jonna, with Mary Straus. *The Healthy Dog Cookbook: 50 Nutritious and Delicious Recipes Your Dog Will Love*. UK: Ivy Press Limited, 2008.

Boneham, Sheila Webster, Ph.D. *The Multiple-Dog Family*. Neptune City: TFH Publications, Inc., 2009.

Boneham, Sheila Webster, Ph.D. *Training Your Dog for Life*. Neptune City: TFH Publications, Inc., 2008.

Dainty, Suellen. *50 Games to Play With Your Dog*. UK: Ivy Press Limited, 2007.

DeVito, Dominique. *Beagles*, Neptune City: TFH Publications, Inc., 2007.

DeVito, Russell-Revesz, Fornino. *World Atlas of Dog Breeds*, 6th Ed. Neptune City: TFH Publications, Inc., 2009.

King, Trish. *Parenting Your Dog: Complete Care and Training for Every Life Stage*. Neptune City: TFH Publications, Inc., 2010.

Knueven, Doug, DVM. *The Holistic Health Guide for Dogs*. Neptune City: TFH Publications, Inc., 2008.

Morgan, Diane. *The Beagle*. Neptune City: TFH Publications, 2005.

Morgan, Diane. *Good Dogkeeping*. Neptune City: TFH Publications, 2005.

Morgan, Diane. *The Living Well Guide for Senior Dogs*. Neptune City: TFH Publications, Inc., 2007.

MAGAZINES
AKC Family Dog
American Kennel Club
260 Madison Avenue
New York, NY 10016
Telephone: (800) 490-5675
E-mail: familydog@akc.org
www.akc.org/pubs/familydog

AKC Gazette
American Kennel Club
260 Madison Avenue
New York, NY 10016
Telephone: (800) 533-7323
E-mail: gazette@akc.org
www.akc.org/pubs/gazette

Dog Fancy
P.O. Box 6050
Mission Viejo, CA 92690-6050
Telephone: (800) 365-4421
E-mail: barkback@dogfancy.com
www.dogfancy.com

Dog & Kennel
Pet Publishing, Inc.
.7-L Dundas Circle
Greensboro, NC 27407
Telephone: (336) 292-4047
Fax: (336) 292-4272
E-mail: info@petpublishing.com
www.dogandkennel.com

Dogs Monthly
Ascot House
High Street, Ascot,
Berkshire, SL5 7JG
United Kingdom
Telephone: 1344 628 269
Fax: 1344 622 771
E-mail: admin@rtc-associates.freeserve.co.uk
www.corsini.co.uk/dogsmonthly

WEBSITES
Beagles on the Web
www.beagles-on-the-web.com

Beagle Rescue, Education, and Welfare
www.brewbeagles.com

Nylabone
www.nylabone.com

TFH Publications, Inc.
www.tfh.com

INDEX

Note: **Boldfaced** numbers indicate illustrations.

PHOTO CREDITS

ABOUT THE AUTHOR

Miriam Fields-Babineau is a graduate of the University of Maryland, with degrees in psychology and zoology. She has been training animals professionally since 1980 and has provided animals for media productions since 1983. Miriam, also an author, has published 39 pet books, numerous magazine and newspaper articles, short stories, and two novels. Her articles have appeared in *Canine Chronicle*, *Dog Fancy*, and *Off Lead*, among other periodicals. She currently writes pet product reviews for the *Examiner* news agency. She lives in Amherst, Virginia. Visit her on the web at www.miriamfields.net.

ABOUT ANIMAL PLANET™

Animal Planet™ is the only television network dedicated exclusively to the connection between humans and animals. The network brings people of all ages together by tapping into our fundamental fascination with animals through an array of fresh programming that includes humor, competition, drama, and spectacle from the animal kingdom.

ABOUT *DOGS 101*

The most comprehensive—and most endearing—dog encyclopedia on television, *DOGS 101* spotlights the adorable, the feisty and the unexpected. A wide-ranging rundown of everyone's favorite dog breeds—from the Dalmatian to Xoloitzcuintli —this series surveys a variety of breeds for their behavioral quirks, genetic history, most famous examples and wildest trivia. Learn which dogs are best for urban living and which would be the best fit for your family. Using a mix of animal experts, pop-culture footage and stylized dog photography, *DOGS 101* is an unprecedented look at man's best friend.